draw manga

STEP-BY-STEP ON YOUR COMPUTER

STEVE & GHY SAMPSON

ILEX

Welcome.

This book will show you, step by step, how to color a manga picture of a girl leaping from a neon-lit city backdrop. To obtain the line art, either download it from the website address on the front cover flap [this is the easiest option], or scan in the images opposite and on page 96.

The first steps will involve coloring in the background areas, such as the buildings, the sky, and all of the signs behind the girl. To begin with, we will create simple, flat areas of color. When the background is complete, we will color the girl as a separate image—again, just using flat areas of color.

The next step will be to join the two images together. Then we'll create special effects, such as adding glows to the neon signs, light in the sky, and lights in the lanterns, and blur selected areas of the picture to add depth. All these effects will be created using a combination of Photoshop effects, filters, and blending modes.

By the end of the book, you will have colored a detailed manga image to a professional standard. The tricks you'll learn along the way will enable you to color your own illustrations to the same level.

Have fun!

This is the first image that we will work on. If you choose to scan rather than download, you will need to do so at high resolution. Our file measures 8.5 x 11.5 inches (22 x 29 cm) at 600 pixels per inch.

First published in the UK in 2007 by
ILEX
The Old Candlemakers
West Street
Lewes
East Sussex
BN7 2NZ

ILEX is an imprint of The Ilex Press Ltd
www.ilex-press.com

Publisher: Alastair Campbell
Creative Director: Peter Bridgewater
Editorial Director: Tom Mugridge
Editor: Ben Renow-Clarke
Art Director: Julie Weir
Design: Jane & Chris Lanaway
Design Assistant: Kate Haynes
Commissioning Editor: Tim Pilcher

British Library Cataloguing-in-Publication
Data: A catalogue record for this book is
available from the British Library

ISBN 13: 978-1-905814-01-5
ISBN 10: 1-905814-01-1

Kimberley font used courtesy of
Ray Larabie. www.larabiefonts.com

Printed and bound in China

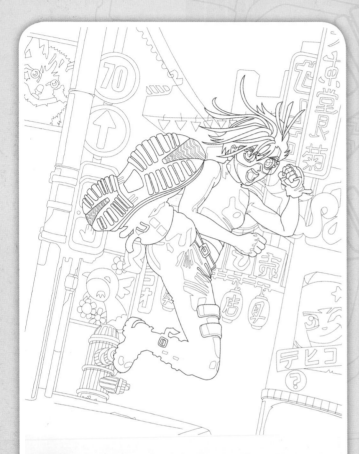

Close and Go To Bridge...	Shift+Ctrl+W
Save	Ctrl+S
Save As...	Shift+Ctrl+S
Save a Version...	

01 The final manga image is made up of two illustrations: One of the girl and the background, and one of just the girl. We've split them up like this to make it easier for you to select and color them, but the techniques we'll cover here are the same as if you were working on a single, flat picture.

Begin by downloading the images from the website address on the front cover flap. Alternatively, you can scan the images from the book. The first image is on page 5, and the second image is on page 96. Just scan the first image for now—you won't need the second one until later in the book. Each scanner will be different, but essentially you should be scanning the image as black and white and at 600 pixels per inch (PPI). Save the first image as Manga_Art.tif.

Once you have the image ready, open it in Photoshop by using the *File > Open* command.

02 Now save the Manga_Art.tif image file in Photoshop as Manga_Art.psd. Go to *File > Save As*, and select *Photoshop* as the *Format*. It may seem odd to be re-saving the file when we haven't done anything to it yet. The reason is that we want the image to be in the Photoshop Document format (PSD) because this format stores all of the layers and effects that some other formats don't.

Layers are a hugely important part of digital imaging, and luckily they're very easy to use. Think of layers as sheets of acetate that can contain different parts of your image—the manga girl and the background, for example. So, you can move the parts separately but when they're stacked one on top of the other they look like they make up one complete image.

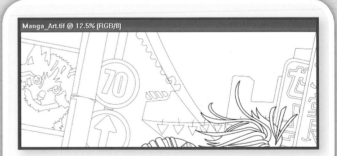

03 Convert the image Manga_Art.psd from Grayscale into RGB using the *Image > Mode > RGB Color* command. You can tell which color mode a picture is in by checking the text in the title bar at the top of the image. In this example, the image has been changed to RGB.

RGB stands for Red Green Blue, and, as that suggests, this mode supports colors—16.8 million of them in fact! This means we'll be able to add as many wild colors and effects to our image as we like. Grayscale mode only supports black, white and shades of gray.

04 Go to the *Layers* palette. If you can't see it on your screen, you'll be able to find it by going to *Window > Layers*. At the bottom of the *Layers* palette is a set of icons, and if you hold your mouse pointer over one of these, a tool tip will appear telling you the name of the icon. Click on the *New Layer* icon (second from the right) and you will see a new layer appear in the palette.

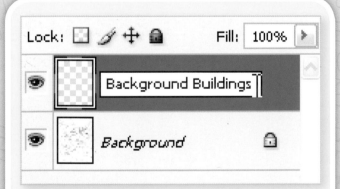

05 At the moment, the new layer will just be called "Layer 1," which will get a bit confusing when you have 20 layers and can't remember what you've put on each one! To get around this, you can rename layers so you know what you've stored on each one. We'll be using this layer for storing the color of the farthest buildings in the background, so we'll call it "Background Buildings."

In the *Layers* palette, double-click on the words "Layer 1." The words will be highlighted and editable. Type in "Background Buildings" and press Return.

06 To choose which layer you want to work on, you need to select it in the *Layers* palette. When a layer is selected, it will be highlighted in blue. Now, click on the "Background" layer to select it.

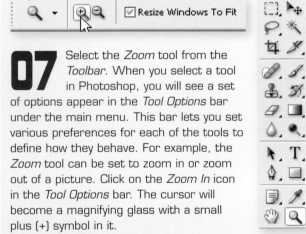

07 Select the *Zoom* tool from the *Toolbar*. When you select a tool in Photoshop, you will see a set of options appear in the *Tool Options* bar under the main menu. This bar lets you set various preferences for each of the tools to define how they behave. For example, the *Zoom* tool can be set to zoom in or zoom out of a picture. Click on the *Zoom In* icon in the *Tool Options* bar. The cursor will become a magnifying glass with a small plus (+) symbol in it.

Next, check the *Resize Windows To Fit* box in the *Tool Options* bar. This means that whenever you zoom in on part of the image, the image window will resize automatically to show you the best view of the piece you are zooming to.

08 Because the image is quite big and we want to be able to select small, detailed areas of it, we need to zoom in to the area that we will be working on. The *Zoom* tool works in two ways: By just clicking with the tool you will zoom in steps centered on the cursor; by clicking and dragging with the tool, you tell Photoshop to zoom in and fill the screen with the area you selected. We will use the second of these behaviors.

Drag a square selection from the top left corner to the sole of the girl's shoe, as shown above. Don't worry about being too precise. When you release the mouse button, Photoshop will zoom in to the selected area.

09 We are now going to start selecting areas of our picture to color. We will build up a selection of all of the areas that will be the same color, and then color them all at the same time.

There are many ways to make selections in Photoshop, but we will use the *Magic Wand* tool. The *Magic Wand* tool works by selecting areas that are the same color, so we will be able to select the white parts of the image that we want to fill, while leaving the black lines alone.

Click on the *Magic Wand* tool in the *Toolbar* to select it. We also need to check the settings in the *Tool Options* bar to make sure they are correct. The *Tolerance* should be set to 32, and the *Anti-alias* and *Contiguous* boxes should both be checked.

TIP If you select the wrong area by mistake, switch to the *Subtract from Selection* option. Then when you click on a selected area, it will be removed from the selection.

New Selection —

Intersect with Selection

Add to Selection

Subtract from Selection

10 Now it's time to make our first selection. With the *Magic Wand* tool ready, click on the background above the cat signpost as shown. When you click, a dotted line will appear to show which area you have selected. This selection line is commonly known as "marching ants" because of the way that the line is animated. We have highlighted the selected area in yellow to make it clearer, but your selection will just have the marching ants around it.

Do not click anywhere else within the image area, because this will deselect the currently selected area.

11 If you wish to scroll around the screen while you are zoomed in, you need to use the *Hand* tool. This can be found next to the *Zoom* tool on the *Toolbar*.

With the *Hand* tool active, you can drag the image around inside the view window without altering any of the elements in the image or affecting the selection.

There is also a shortcut to allow you to use the *Hand* tool while you have another tool selected. Switch to the *Move* tool on the *Toolbar* and you'll see that the cursor is a black arrow as normal. Press the Spacebar, and the cursor will temporarily change to a hand, indicating that it is now acting as the *Hand* tool. Scroll around the screen to check. When you release the Spacebar, the cursor will switch back to the *Move* tool.

13 Now we have two areas selected, let's zoom out of the image to get an idea of how much is left to go.

Go to the *Toolbar* and select the *Zoom* tool. This tool also has options available in the *Tool Options* bar. We used the tool set to *Zoom In* mode before (the magnifying glass with the plus icon), but this time we want to use the *Zoom Out* mode. To access this, click on the magnifying glass with the minus icon on it. Just like using the tool in the other mode, you can now click on the image to zoom out.

You'll see that there is still a lot of the background left to select!

12 It's now time to add the next part of the background to the selection. Use the *Hand* tool to move the image around until you can see the background below the cat sign.

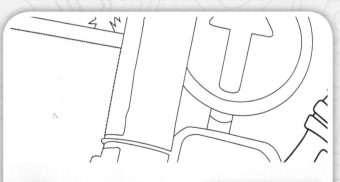

Switch to the *Magic Wand* tool and go to the *Tool Options* bar. Make sure that the *Add to Selection* option is selected. This means that the new selection area will be added to the old one. Click in the area beneath the cat sign—as pictured—to add it to the selection.

14 Switch back to *Zoom In* mode, and zoom in to the area next to the fire hydrant and the robin sign. Use the *Hand* tool to pan around the image if necessary (remember the Spacebar shortcut).

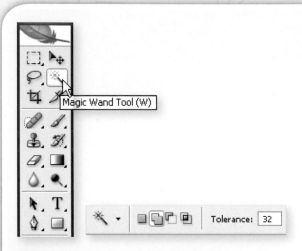

15 Switch to the *Magic Wand* tool and make sure that the *Add to Selection* option is selected in the *Tool Options* bar.

17 The next area is just to the right of the previous one—immediately to the left of the fire hydrant.
    As you click in each area, you should see more marching ants appear. If the original marching ants disappear, then you haven't set the tool options correctly. Check that *Add to Selection* is highlighted. You may need to go back and start the selection process again if the options weren't set correctly.

16 Select the small area to the left of the robin sign as shown above.

18 The next selection to be made is the small area between the fire hydrant and the girl's boot. Click in it with the *Magic Wand* tool to add it to the selection.

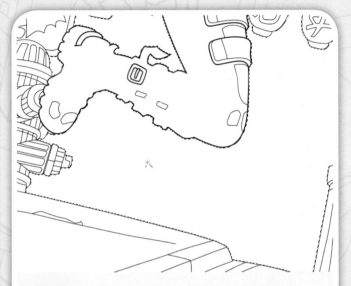

20 The next area to select is the large piece of background space to the right of the girl's leg. This will select everything from the street up to the lanterns.

19 Next, click on the area of background between the girl's leg and the signs to add it to the selection.

21 After that selection, we'll need to scroll around the image so we can clearly see the next area that needs to be selected. The previous selection didn't catch the small area between the girl's leg and the lantern on the left, so use the *Hand* tool to pan around the image until you can clearly see the required area.

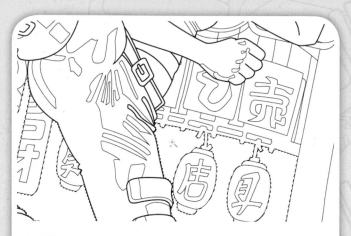

22 Switch back to the *Magic Wand* tool (or release the Spacebar if you used the shortcut) and make sure the tool is set to *Add to Selection* mode. Click on the area between the girl's leg and the lantern to add it to the selection.

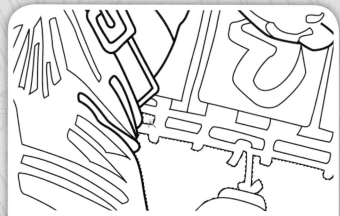

24 Switch back to the *Magic Wand* tool. Click in the first of the small gaps next to the girl's leg to add it to the selection. Now would be a good time to save the selection using *Select > Save Selection*. You can either create a new channel, or add it to the previous one. If you're happy that the selection is all okay, then it's a better idea to add it to the previous channel than to create a new one.

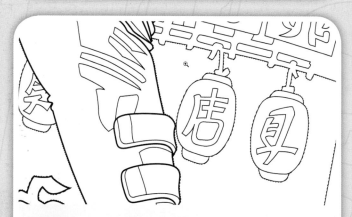

23 Next, we will be selecting the small areas that the lanterns are hanging from. To make sure that you can select them cleanly, you will need to zoom in to the image. Switch to the *Zoom* tool and drag out a zoom area enclosing all of the background gaps.

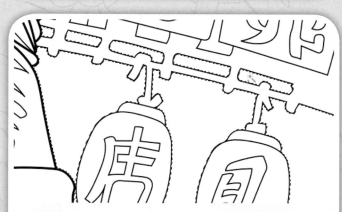

25 Still using the *Magic Wand* tool, select the remaining four small background areas above the hanging lanterns.

26 It's time to zoom out and move around the image again before we make our next selection. This time, rather than going all the way to the *Toolbar* to switch tools, try using a keyboard shortcut.

Hold down the Control (Ctrl) key—or the Command (Cmd) key if you are working on a Mac—and press minus (-). This zooms out of the image. Press it again to zoom farther out. You can now use the Spacebar shortcut to pan around the image.

28 We now need to pan around the image again. Switch to the *Hand* tool either by using the *Toolbar* or the Spacebar keyboard shortcut. Pan up and across the image until you can see the small area above the girl's boot and between the signposts as shown.

27 Move across the image until you can see the background area just below the girl's outstretched foot, and just above the robin sign. You can zoom in again by using a similar keyboard shortcut to before, but this time hold Ctrl/Cmd and press plus (+)—it's on the same key as the equals sign.

When you're ready, click on the background area with the *Magic Wand* tool to add it to the selection.

29 Click in the first area—directly below and to the left of the arrow sign—with the *Magic Wand* tool to add it to the selection.
Next, pan up the image a little, and add the gap between the arrow sign and the 70 sign to the selection.
Finally, pan up a little more, and add the gap above and to the left of the 70 sign to the selection as shown.

30 After those three small selections, we can now make one large one. With the *Magic Wand* tool selected, click in the background area of the building to the right of the signs and above the girl's shoe to add it to the selection.

Now would be a good time to save the selection again. Go to *Select > Save Selection*, and select the channel from the drop-down list to replace the existing channel with the new selection.

32 There is still one tiny piece of the roof that we haven't selected yet. Zoom in on the area where the telephone wire intersects the roof and you'll see a small gap. Zoom right in on this gap as close as you can go—the farthest Photoshop can zoom is to 1600%.

Select the gap using the *Magic Wand* tool. You may have to make more than one selection to include all of the white areas.

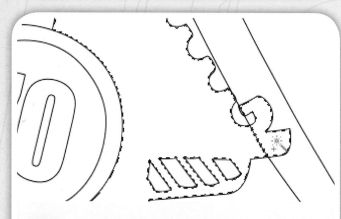

31 You'll notice that a telephone wire cuts across the last area that we selected, meaning that a small area of the roof wasn't selected. Remedy that now by zooming into the image and clicking in the roof area with the *Magic Wand* tool.

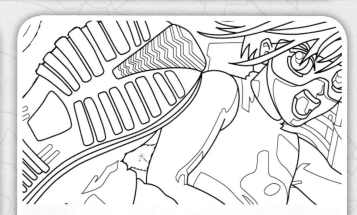

33 Zoom out of the image again so you can see the whole illustration. If you press Ctrl/Cmd+0 (zero), Photoshop will zoom out automatically to fit the whole image onto the screen.

Zoom in on the area between the girl's right boot and her right arm. Make sure you're using the *Magic Wand* tool in *Add to Selection* mode, then click in the small area of background next to the girl's arm.

34 There are two more background building areas next to the girl's head. Pan across the image using the *Hand* tool until you can see the area between the girl's foot and her hair.

Click on the area between the toe of her boot and the tips of her hair with the *Magic Wand* tool to add it to the selection. Next, pan up the image slightly (remember, holding the Spacebar temporarily enables the *Hand* tool), then click in the building area above the girl's head to add it to the selection.

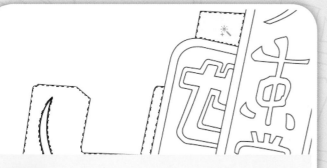

35 There is another part of this background building just above the signs in the top-right corner of the image. Pan to the top of the sign containing Japanese characters to the right of the girl's head. With the *Magic Wand* tool, click inside this building area to add it to the selection.

36 Zoom all the way out of the image, either by using the *Zoom* tool or the keyboard shortcut Ctrl/Cmd+0 (zero). Next, we will be working in detail around the girl's hair, so select the *Zoom* tool and click and drag an area enclosing the girl's head, as shown.

Now would be a good time to save the selection. Use the *Select > Save Selection* command, and overwrite your existing selection. You should also save the image using the *File > Save* command.

37 Switch to the *Magic Wand* tool in *Add to Selection* mode, and click on the three small background building areas that lie between the strands of the girl's hair directly above her ear.

39 Now zoom back out of the image until you can see the strands of the girl's hair again. Pan across the image and add the small triangle between the strands of hair as shown.

38 There is one more tiny area to be selected in this part of the image. Zoom in as far as possible on the top-right corner of the largest of the previous selections, and you will see a small gap. Click inside this gap with the *Magic Wand* tool to add it to the selection.

40 Now pan across the image to the right a little and use the *Magic Wand* tool to add the two small background areas alongside the next strand of hair.

41 That's the area above the hair done. Zoom out of the image, then drag and zoom in again on the area around the girl's ear.

43 Next, pan across the image to the area just beneath the girl's left eye, as shown.

42 There is a small area between two strands of hair that wasn't added to the previous selection that we made. With the *Magic Wand* tool set to *Add to Selection* mode, click in the small triangular background area.

44 There is another small triangle of background here between the girl's cheek and the sign. Click in the area with the *Magic Wand* tool to add it to the selection.

Now would be a good time to save the selection using the *Select > Save Selection* command. Again, choose to save over your current selection. Also, be sure to save the image itself using *File > Save*.

45 You'll notice that there is another tiny area above the previous selection that wasn't added previously. Zoom in on the area up to the maximum 1600% so that you can see it clearly, then click in it with the *Magic Wand* tool to add it to the selection.

46 Zoom out until you can see the whole of the picture. Again, you can either use the *Zoom* tool; the single-step zoom keyboard shortcut, Ctrl/Cmd+- (minus); or the full zoom shortcut, Ctrl/Cmd+O (zero).

47 We have now selected all the areas where the background buildings are showing. In Photoshop, you can quickly highlight a selected area by using a "quick mask." This can be switched on and off with one button on the *Toolbar*, and is a very good way of quickly previewing selections.

The *Quick Mask* button is located directly below the color buttons on the *Toolbar*. The right of the two buttons turns the quick mask on, and the left turns it off. Click on the right button and the selected area will be shown in white, while the rest of the image is colored red. Your image should look like the one shown here.

49

Now we've finished making the selections from the Background layer, we need to switch to the Background Buildings layer in preparation for coloring. Remember that in Photoshop, any work you do on an image will affect the active layer only. To change the active layer, you simply need to click on it in the *Layers* palette.

Go to the *Layers* palette (select *Window > Layers* if you can't see it) and click on the Background Buildings layer. It should change color to show that it is now the active layer.

50

Now it's time to pick the color that we will use for the background buildings. There are several ways to select colors in Photoshop, but we will use the *Color Picker*.

To access the *Color Picker*, click on the *Set Foreground Color* button—the large square of color beneath the tools in the *Toolbar*. This will open the *Color Picker* in a new window.

You can select a color simply by clicking on it in the rainbow-colored box at the left of the *Color Picker*, but we'll enter the numerical values of the color to get a precise match. We'll use the RGB color values (see TIP box for more on this). Enter 75 in the R: box, 0 in the G: box, and 73 in the B: box, then click *OK*. You should now have a dark purple as the foreground color.

48

If there are any areas missing from your selection, switch back to standard edit mode by clicking the left *Quick Mask* button. This will turn off the red overlay and go back to the normal marching ants selection shape. Use the *Magic Wand* tool to add any missing areas, then switch back to *Quick Mask* mode to preview the change. When you're happy with the selection, switch back to *Standard Edit* mode.

TIP

It may seem odd at first to think of colors in terms of numbers, but really it's quite straightforward. It's all based on mixing primary colors, and the numbers represent the amount of each primary color that needs to be added to make the final color. Computer screens use the three primary colors red, green, and blue (hence RGB). If all of these colors are set to 0 then you will have black, and if you apply them all at 100%, you will have white.

Expand Selection ✕

Expand By: 5 pixels

OK

Cancel

51 Before we fill the selection with color, there's still something we can do to improve it. At the moment, we have selected all of the white space between the black lines, but it would be good to remove some of the background lines too. This will mean that the background blends together better, and ultimately, this will help the girl to stand out from the background.

We can achieve this by expanding the selection by a small amount so that when we fill the selection with color it will cover over the background lines. Go to *Select > Modify > Expand*. Most of the lines in the image are about 5 pixels wide, so enter a value of 5 into the *Expand Selection* window and click *OK*.

52 To see what we have just done more clearly, click once on the *Quick Mask* icon at the bottom of the *Toolbar*. If you zoom into the image, you will now see that the red mask no longer covers the black lines of the background buildings. When you're done, click back on the *Edit in Standard Mode* button to return to the normal selection view. Use the Ctrl/Cmd+O (zero) shortcut to zoom back out to view the whole image on the screen.

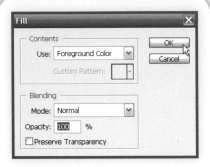

Fill ✕

Contents

Use: Foreground Color

Custom Pattern:

Blending

Mode: Normal

Opacity: 100 %

☐ Preserve Transparency

OK

Cancel

53 At last, it's time to add our first color to the image! Make sure that the Background Buildings layer is selected, and that the marching ants selection is visible on the screen. Next, go to *Edit > Fill*. This will bring up the *Fill* dialog box.

There are a few settings in this dialog box that we must be sure are correct. Set the *Use* drop-down menu to *Foreground Color*. This means that the selection will be filled with the currently selected dark purple color. Next, make sure that the *Blending Mode* is set to *Normal* and the *Opacity* is at 100%. When all that is done, click *OK*.

54 The background buildings should now all be filled with color. With that done, we no longer require the selection. Use the keyboard shortcut Ctrl/Cmd+D to deselect the selection. The marching ants will disappear to show that there is no longer anything selected.

55 Zoom into the image to check the fill lines. You should see that the color fill runs over the top of the black background building lines. When you're happy with it, save the image by going to *File > Save*, or by using the Ctrl/Cmd+S keyboard shortcut.

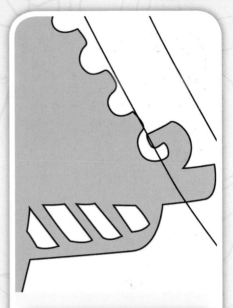

57 The opacity controls can be found in the *Layers* palette. Select the Background Buildings layer by clicking on it, and then either type directly into the *Opacity* box, or click on the arrow to bring up a slider, and change the layer's opacity to 35%. You'll notice when you do so that the color of the layer becomes lighter, but the black lines on the layer below remain solid black. The beauty of doing it this way is that you can always turn the layer's opacity back up if you want to preview the final color, and then down again when you want to resume work on the image.

56 The color is correct for the final image, but it is so dark that it's hard to see what else is going on in the image, and we can't see the lines we need for our subsequent selections. Rather than change this to a lighter color, we can lower the opacity of the Background Buildings layer, meaning that we will be able to see through the layer to the lines below. This will all become clear in the next step. For now, zoom in on the part of the image where the telephone wires cross the colored roof.

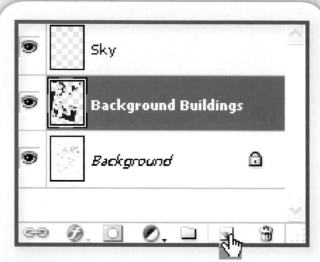

58 It's now time to create a new layer to start a new selection for coloring. Make sure that the Background Buildings layer is selected in the *Layers* palette, then click the *Create a New Layer* button at the bottom of the palette. This will create a new layer above the Background Buildings layer.

Double-click on the name of this new layer to rename it. Name this layer "Sky." As you can no doubt guess, we will use this layer for coloring all of the sky areas in the image.

60 Make sure that the Sky layer is selected in the *Layers* palette, and that you can see the area where the telephone wires run past the roof. Then, using the *Magic Wand* tool, click in the area between the phone lines and the roof. Because *Sample All Layers* is turned on in the *Magic Wand* options, a selection will be created following the pen lines in the image.

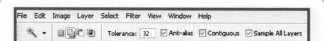

59 Switch to the *Magic Wand* tool in the *Toolbar*. As before, make sure that the tool is set to *Add to Selection* mode by clicking the appropriate button in the *Tool Options* bar. This time, check the *Sample All Layers* box too. This means that when you click on an area with the *Magic Wand* tool, it will check through all of the visible layers before calculating the selection, rather than just using the layer that you are currently working on.

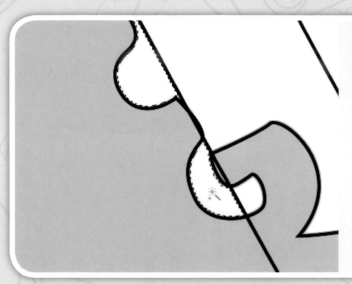

61 Zoom in to the image a bit more if you need to so that you can see the small area of sky below the previous selection. Click in this area with the *Magic Wand* tool to add it to the selection. If you find that the previous selection has now been deselected, then check to make sure that *Add to Selection* is enabled in the *Tool Options* bar. If it wasn't enabled, you'll have to make the selection from the previous step again as well as this one.

62 The next area to select is immediately to the right of the previous area—just the other side of the telephone wire. Click in this small area with the *Magic Wand* tool to add it to the selection.

63 We'll now add the large area of sky beneath the roof. Pan down the image a bit using the *Hand* tool or the Spacebar keyboard shortcut. Click in the area of sky beneath the curve of the roof to add it to the sky selection.

Now would be a good time to save the selection we've made so far. Go to *Select > Save Selection*. We no longer require the building selection that we saved before, so you can safely save over it with this new selection. This will keep the file size down and means that you won't have a confusing list of selections to choose from next time you come to load one. Save the image as well by going to *File > Save*.

64 Next, pan down the image a little more using the *Hand* tool. The next area to be selected is directly beneath the previous one. Using the *Magic Wand* tool, click in the large area of sky beneath the triangular flags to add it to the selection.

66 We'll need to zoom in for the next selection, so switch to the *Zoom* tool and zoom in to the tiny triangular area to the right of our previous selection. When you can see it clearly, switch back to the *Magic Wand* tool in *Add to Selection* mode and click to add the sky to our selection.
  When you're done, zoom out again a little so that you can see the string of flags and the girl's hair.

65 The next area to select is the small piece of sky bordered by one of the flags, the hair, and the telephone wire. Click in this area with the *Magic Wand* tool to add it to the selection.

67 The next area of sky to add is above and slightly to the left of the last selection. It's the small area just above the flag. Click in it with the *Magic Wand* to add it to the selection.

68 Pan up the image and slightly to the right until you can see the area of sky above our previous selection, and just below the girl's hair. Click in this area with the *Magic Wand* tool to add it to the selection. There are still a few more small areas of sky to select before we can start adding our next color.

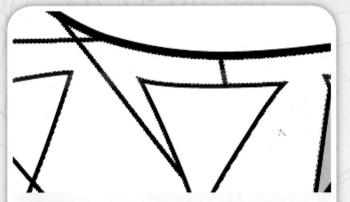

70 Next, pan to the right of the image and add the two sky areas beside the next triangular flag to the selection by clicking in them with the *Magic Wand* tool.

69 We can quickly deal with the remaining sky areas in this part of the image. First, add the large area next to the triangular flag, then switch to the *Zoom* tool and zoom in closer to select the tiny area next to the strand of the girl's hair.

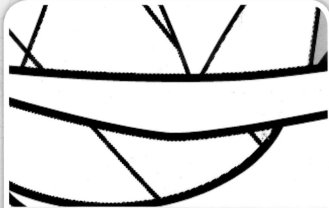

71 The next two sky areas to be added to the selection are directly below the previous two. The first is the large section between the telephone wires and the strands of the girl's hair, and the second is the smaller triangular selection to the right of it. You may need to zoom in a little on the image to be able to see the smaller section clearly.

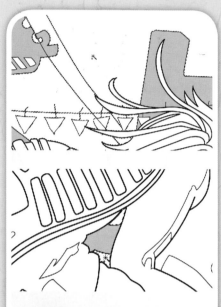

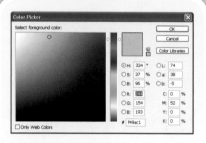

72 Zoom out of the image, using either the *Zoom* tool or the keyboard shortcut Ctrl/Cmd+- (minus) until you can see the majority of the image. After those tricky areas of sky, we'll now add a couple of large areas.

Switch back to the *Magic Wand* tool in *Add to Selection* mode and click in the area between the two telephone wires. Next, click in the main area of sky to the right of the wires to add that to the selection.

Finally, pan down to the girl's boot and click on the two remaining sky areas just below her boot and next to her right arm with the *Magic Wand* tool to add them to the sky selection.

73 That should be the entire sky area selected. You can check this by switching to *Quick Mask* mode to easily see which areas are selected.

Zoom out of the image so that you can see the whole picture. The quickest way to do this is to use the Ctrl/Cmd+O (zero) keyboard shortcut. Now, click on the *Edit in Quick Mask Mode* button at the bottom of the *Toolbar*. This will color the areas that aren't part of the selection red. Make sure that your image looks like the one shown and that all of the correct areas are selected. If not, switch back to *Standard Edit* mode and add the missing areas using the *Magic Wand* tool.

74 When you are happy that you have selected all of the sky areas, switch back to *Standard Edit* mode by pressing the *Edit in Standard Mode* button at the bottom of the *Toolbar*, or by pressing Q on the keyboard.

We'll now choose the color for the sky. Click on the *Set Foreground Color* button in the *Toolbar* (the large square of color at the bottom) to open the *Color Picker*. As before, we'll enter RGB values into the *Color Picker* to make sure we get an exact color. Enter R: 244, G: 154, B: 193. You should have a pale pink color. Click *OK* to make this the foreground color.

75 Now we can fill the sky selection with the new color. Make sure the Sky layer is selected in the *Layers* palette, then go to *Edit > Fill* and check that the options are set to *Use*: *Foreground Color*, *Mode*: *Normal*, and *Opacity*: 100%. When you click *OK*, the sky should fill with pink. We no longer need the sky selection, so use the Ctrl/Cmd+D keyboard shortcut to deselect it.

76 Now that we have the sky color in place, we can switch the background buildings back to their full color to get a better idea of how the image is looking.

Go to the *Layers* palette and click on the Background Buildings layer. At the moment, its opacity is set to 35%, so either type into the box or click on the arrow next to it and drag the slider to set the layer's opacity to 100%. We can now see our picture beginning to take shape.

77 We'll now turn our attention to the buildings on the right of the image. As usual, we'll be adding the color to these buildings on a separate layer, so go to the *Layers* palette. New layers are always created on the layer immediately above the currently selected layer. We want this new layer to be above the Background Buildings layer but below the Sky layer, so click on the Background Buildings layer to select it.

Now, click on the *Create a New Layer* button found at the bottom of the *Layers* palette to create a new layer below the Sky layer.

78 Next, we need to rename the layer. Double-click on the new layer's name in the *Layers* palette and give it the name "Right-hand Building."

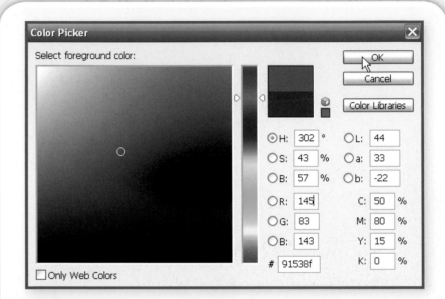

80 Now that the *Paint Bucket* tool is set up correctly, we need to pick a color to use for filling the building areas.

Click on the *Set Foreground Color* button at the bottom of the *Toolbar* to open the *Color Picker*. Again, we'll be entering numerical color values to choose an exact color. Enter R: 145, G: 83, B: 143 into the *Color Picker* and click *OK*. This gives you a muted purple foreground color.

79 We'll use a different tool to fill the areas of this building with color. Rather than selecting areas individually and filling them all with color at once, we'll use the *Paint Bucket* tool to fill areas individually. This gives more instant feedback on how the image is looking, but it makes it more difficult to go back and alter areas if you make any mistakes. Don't worry, though, we won't let that happen!

Click on the *Paint Bucket* tool in the *Toolbar*. It's near the center of the tool set, and shares a space with the *Gradient* tool. If the *Gradient* tool is visible,

click and hold the cursor on it until a menu pops up enabling you to select the *Paint Bucket* tool.

We also need to check the *Tool Options* bar to make sure that the settings are correct. Set them to the following: *Foreground*; *Mode*: *Normal*; *Opacity* 100%; *Tolerance*: 32; *Anti-alias*: checked; *Contiguous*: checked; *All Layers*: checked. The *All Layers* setting works in a similar way to the *Use All Layers* setting on the *Magic Wand* tool. It means that Photoshop will examine the edges of all of the layers before making the fill on the current layer.

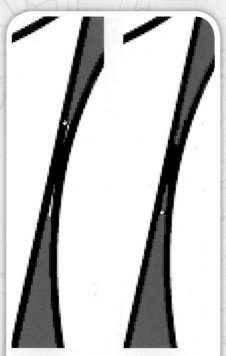

81 It's now time to fill our first area with color using the *Paint Bucket* tool. Make sure that the Right-hand Building layer is selected in the *Layers* palette and pan over to the right side of the image. Click in the area to the right of the topmost neon sign, as shown, to fill it with color.

You'll notice that all the colors that we have used so far are very similar in tone. This is important for setting the mood of the piece, and will be useful when we come to add our special effects to the image later, and we need the background areas to blend together.

83 If you zoom in close to the point where the two previously filled areas meet, you will notice that there are some white gaps where the fill didn't quite go all the way to the black lines. We can correct this by adding more color with the *Paint Bucket* tool.

Zoom in as close as possible, and then click on the white areas with the *Paint Bucket* tool. The "hotspot" of the cursor icon is the tip of the paint that's falling out of the bucket. Make sure that this is over the white area before you click. If you make a mistake, use the Ctrl/Cmd+Z keyboard shortcut to undo and try again.

82 We'll now continue to fill sections of the building in the same area of the image. Zoom into the area just below the neon sign and to the right of the girl's left hand. Click on the right of the two thin background shapes to fill it with color, and then pan down a little and click on the next section where the shape continues after the girl's glove.

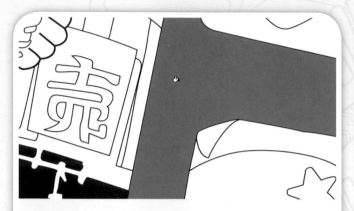

84 We can now fill the large area directly beneath the neon sign. Zoom out of the image, then zoom in again until you can see the area around the poster with the girl's face on it.

Click once with the *Paint Bucket* tool in the area above the poster to fill it with color.

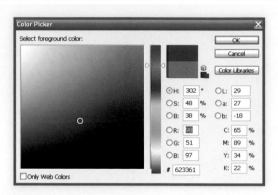

86 Click on the *Set Foreground Color* button at the bottom of the *Toolbar* to bring up the *Color Picker*. As usual, we will enter an RGB value into the *Color Picker* to make sure the exact color is chosen.

Enter R: 98, G: 51, B: 97 into the *Color Picker*. The foreground color should now be a darker shade of purple than the one we were using previously.

85 Another area just below the previous one also needs to be colored. Pan down the image so you can see the area below the bar that's beneath the question mark. Click in this area with the *Paint Bucket* tool to fill it with color.

That's all of this building that needs to be filled with this color. We'll fill the rest of the building with a different color.

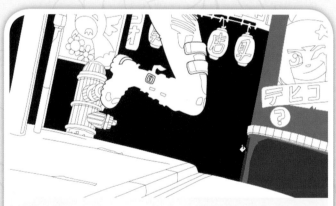

87 With the new color set up and ready, make sure that you have the *Paint Bucket* tool selected, and pan over to the white area next to our previous selection.

Click once with the *Paint Bucket* tool in the large area at the bottom of the building, then once more in the thin area to the left of it, to fill them both with the new dark purple color.

88 We are now going to focus on filling in the small rectangular areas of the bar immediately above our last selection. Switch to the *Zoom* tool, or use the Ctrl/Cmd++ (plus) keyboard shortcut, and zoom in on the leftmost of these rectangles. Switch back to the *Paint Bucket* tool and click in the rectangle to fill it with color.

90 We'll now pick a new color to fill the blank squares above the rectangles that we just filled. Click on the *Set Foreground Color* button at the bottom of the *Toolbar* to bring up the *Color Picker*. Enter R: 182, G: 153, B: 181 in the *Color Picker* and click *OK*. You should now have a pale purple foreground color.

89 Now, continue panning across the image and clicking with the *Paint Bucket* tool until all of the small rectangles are filled. You may find it useful to use the keyboard shortcut key G, holding the Spacebar to temporarily switch to the *Hand* tool when you want to move across the image.

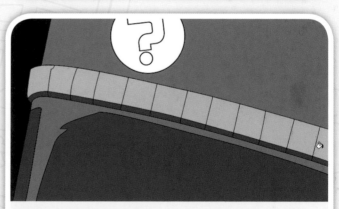

91 Using the Paint Bucket tool, click once on each of the 12 squares to fill them all with our new paler purple color.

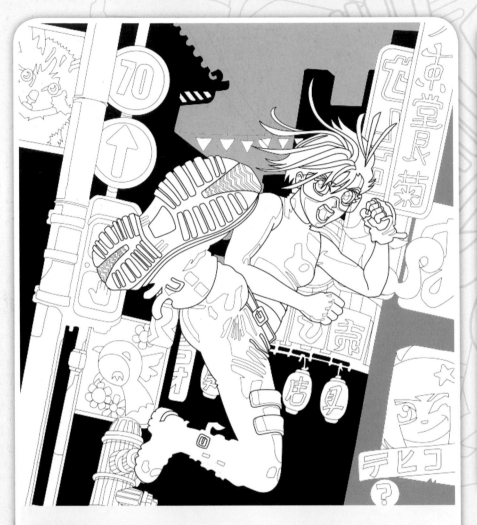

93 Now that the Right-hand Building colors are complete, we can start on our next area. We'll focus on the sidewalk next.

With the Right-hand Building layer still selected in the *Layers* palette, click on the *Create a New Layer* button at the bottom of the palette. Double-click on the name of the new layer and rename it "Sidewalk+Street."

92 Zoom out of the image so you can see the whole picture—use the Ctrl/Cmd+O (zero) keyboard shortcut. Looking at the image now with a lot of our background colors blocked in, we can see that the newly colored building is blending into the background buildings a little too well. We need to make it stand out a bit more.

Because we stored all of the color information on a separate layer, we can simply alter the color balance of the entire layer, rather than going back and refilling all of the individual sections with a new color.

Go to *Image > Adjustments > Hue/Saturation*. This will bring up the *Hue/Saturation* dialog box. See the Tip box opposite for more information on this dialog box.

Either enter numbers directly into the boxes, or adjust the sliders to the following settings: *Hue*: +40, *Saturation*: -20, *Lightness*: +20. This will make all of the colors on the Right-hand Building layer change by the same amount, and make them stand out from the background buildings.

TIP There are three main settings in the *Hue/ Saturation* dialog box: *Hue*, *Saturation*, and *Lightness*.

Hue is a more accurate term for what most people would call color—for example green, blue, and red are all different hues.

The Saturation is the intensity, or strength, of the color—for example a pale, pastel red as opposed to a deep, vibrant red.

Lightness controls the amount of light in the color—for example a dark, almost black, red as opposed to a bright, light red.

94

Next, we'll pick up the same color that we used on the wall of the right-hand building and use that to color the sidewalk. You can very easily pick up a color from anywhere in an image by using the *Eyedropper* tool. This can be found near the bottom of the *Toolbar*.

Select the *Eyedropper* tool and click on the right-hand building wall next to the poster of the girl to pick up that color. You will immediately see the foreground color change in the *Toolbar* to show the new color that you just picked up.

95

We can now start filling areas with our new color. Switch to the *Paint Bucket* tool and make sure the Sidewalk+Street layer is selected in the *Layers* palette.

Zoom in on the bottom part of the image so that you can see the sidewalk in the bottom-left corner. Click once with the *Paint Bucket* tool on the main area of the sidewalk to fill it with our new color. Next, move to the right a little and click on the front edge of each curb stone to color it.

96

Next, we'll pick another color from the wall of the right-hand building. Pan over to the right and switch to the *Eyedropper* tool—if you have one of the painting tools selected, such as the *Paint Bucket*, then you can hold the Alt/Option key down to temporarily switch to the *Eyedropper* tool. Click on the lightest color that we used for the square bricks on the wall.

Pan back over to the sidewalk and switch to the *Paint Bucket* tool. Click on the top of the three curb stones to fill them with the lighter color.

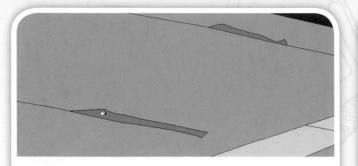

97 Now, pan back over to the right-hand building and use the *Eyedropper* tool to pick up the darkest color that we used for the building. The large area right at the bottom is probably the easiest place to pick the color from. With the color now set as your foreground color, pan back over to the sidewalk.

Switch back to the *Paint Bucket* tool and use it to fill the two cracks in the sidewalk with the darker color.

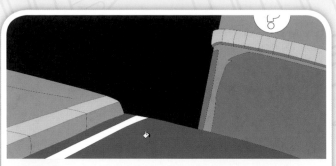

99 With the *Paint Bucket* selected, click on the largest area of the street to fill it with the new color. Next, click on the thin part of the street next to the sidewalk to fill it with color.

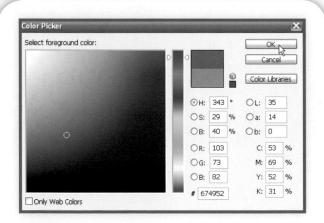

98 We've now finished with the sidewalk, but we'll color in the street on the same layer. First, though, we'll pick a new color for it. Click on the *Set Foreground Color* button at the bottom of the *Toolbar* to bring up the *Color Picker*. Enter R: 103, G: 73, B: 82 and click *OK*. You should now have a dark purple-brown set as your foreground color.

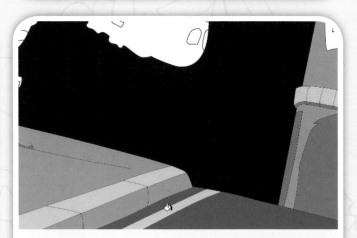

100 We'll make the street marking the same color as the light edge of the curb. Switch to the *Eyedropper* tool (remember, you can use the Alt/Option key keyboard shortcut) and sample the lightest color at the top edge of the curb.

Switch back to the *Paint Bucket* and use the new color to fill the line marked on the street.

102 Click on the Background Buildings layer in the *Layers* palette to select it. Next, go to *Image > Adjustments > Hue/Saturation* to bring up the *Hue/Saturation* dialog box. Using either the sliders or by typing directly into the box, enter *Hue*: +20, *Saturation*: -20, *Lightness*: +20, then click *OK*. The color of the background buildings is now closer to the other colors in the image, which will be better for us to work with later on.

101 Now we've finished with the street and the sidewalk, zoom out so you can see the entire image. The easiest way to do this is to use the Ctrl/Cmd+0 (zero) keyboard shortcut. The image is really starting to come together now, but before we go any further, we can alter the colors slightly to give them a better balance.

Again, we will use Photoshop's *Hue/Saturation* controls to alter all of the colors on a layer at the same time. The background buildings are too powerful at the moment, so we can tone them down a bit.

103 We'll now do the same with the Sky layer to tone it down to fit with the rest of the colors in the image.

Click on the Sky layer in the *Layers* palette to select it. Go to *Image > Adjustments > Hue/Saturation* again to bring up the *Hue/Saturation* dialog box. This time, enter the following settings: *Hue*: +20, *Saturation*: -20, *Lightness* +20, then click *OK*. The sky will now be a less intense, orangey pink.

Close	Ctrl+W
Close All	Alt+Ctrl+W
Close and Go To Bridge...	Shift+Ctrl+W
Save	Ctrl+S
Save As...	Shift+Ctrl+S
Save a Version...	
Save for Web...	Alt+Shift+Ctrl+S
Revert	F12

104 Now that we've got the colors in the image at a satisfactory balance, it's a good idea to save the picture. Go to *File > Save*, or use the Ctrl/Cmd+S keyboard shortcut.
  It makes sense to save your work often, and it's good practice to do so before you leave your computer for a length of time, or before starting up additional applications while you are working on the file.

106 Pan up to the top left of the image where the roof meets the sky. Switch to the *Paint Bucket* tool and fill the four small blank areas on the underside of the roof with the new foreground color.

105 Click on the Background Buildings layer in the *Layers* palette to select it. Zoom in slightly on the right-hand building and use the *Eyedropper* tool to pick up the main wall color of the right-hand building.

107 Zoom out so that you can see the whole of the image again. The next area we are going to be working on contains the two hanging lanterns below the girl's right arm.
  Zoom in so that you can clearly see the lanterns and the bar that they are hanging from on your screen. The easiest way to do this is to switch to the *Zoom* tool and drag a rectangle around the desired area.

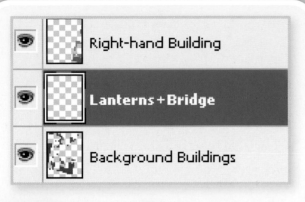

108 Before we start work on the new area, we'll create a layer for it to go on. With the *Background Buildings* layer selected, click on the *Create a New Layer* icon at the bottom of the *Layers* palette. Double-click on the name of the new layer in the *Layers* palette and rename it "Lanterns+Bridge."

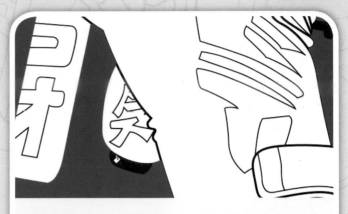

110 There is another lantern at the other side of the girl's leg. Pan to the left of the image so you can see the lantern, and fill its bottom section with the same color.

109 Click on the *Set Foreground Color* button on the *Toolbar* to open up the *Color Picker*. Enter R: 62, G: 25, B: 48 into the *Color Picker* and click *OK*. This will give you a very dark purple color.

Make sure that the Lanterns+Bridge layer is selected. Switch to the *Paint Bucket* tool and click on the bar that the lanterns are hanging from to fill it with our new dark color. Click on the top and bottom sections of both lanterns to fill them with the same color.

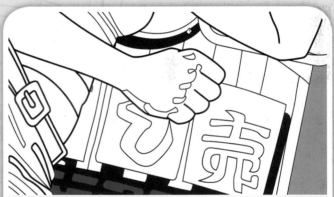

111 Pan up and to the right (remember: you can hold down the Spacebar to temporarily switch to the *Hand* tool) until you can see the area just above the girl's right hand.

Using the *Paint Bucket* tool, fill the three top sections of the bridge directly above the girl's hand.

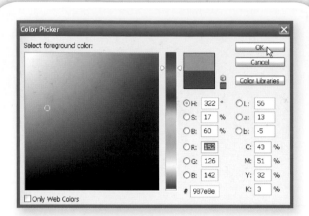

112 That's all of the dark bridge and lantern areas finished. We now need to select a new color to carry on filling.

Click on the *Set Foreground Color* button at the bottom of the *Toolbar* to bring up the *Color Picker*. Enter R: 152, G: 126, B: 142 into the *Color Picker* and click *OK*. You should now have a lighter shade of purple as your foreground color.

114 We'll now carry on filling the bridge paneling with the same color. Pan down a bit using the *Hand* tool so that you can see the bottom of the bridge where the lanterns are hanging from. Switch to the *Paint Bucket* tool and fill in all of the gaps between the Japanese characters on the bridge. You may need to zoom in slightly to fill the smallest of these gaps next to the girl's belt.

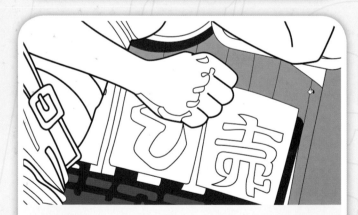

113 We will use this color to fill some more of the bridge behind the girl's hand. Click in each of the upright sections of the bridge above and to the right of her hand and use the *Paint Bucket* to fill them with color.

115 The next area of the bridge that needs filling is near the girl's head. Use the *Hand* tool, or the Spacebar keyboard shortcut, to pan up the image until you can see the girl's head.

Switch to the *Paint Bucket* tool, and fill the two areas of bridge paneling next to the girl's chin.

116 There are two more tiny areas of bridge that need coloring. Zoom in close on the girl's chin, and you should be able to see one small area at either side of her chin. Fill both of these using the *Paint Bucket* tool.

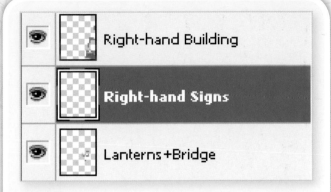

118 We're done with the Lanterns+Bridge layer for now, so it's time to create a new layer for our next area of coloring.

Go to the *Layers* palette and click the *Create a New Layer* button. This layer will be used to color the signs on the right of the image, so double-click on the layer's name and rename it as "Right-hand Signs."

117 Using either the *Zoom* tool or the Ctrl/Cmd+- (minus) keyboard shortcut, zoom out from the face so that you can see some more of the image.

Switch to the *Eyedropper* tool and pick the darkest color that was used on the bridge, just below the girl's arm.

We'll now use this color to fill the top of the bridge. Zoom in again so you can see the detail in the image, and pan over to the area just to the right of the girl's mouth.

Use the *Paint Bucket* tool to fill the small area of the bridge as shown. Now would be a good time to save your image using *File > Save*.

119 We'll fill the signs using colors that will help later when we come back to add glowing neon effects to them.

For the first sign, we'll use the same dark color that we just used for the bridge. Make sure you are on the Right-hand Signs layer and select the *Paint Bucket* tool. Click in the sign above the girl's head to fill it.

121 Keeping the same color and still on the Right-hand Signs layer, move down the image a little and use the *Paint Bucket* to fill the two sign areas below the girl's hand.

120 Zoom in and carry on filling the gaps in the sign. Don't forget to fill inside the Japanese characters. There should be another six spaces to fill above the girl's arm.

122 Next, zoom in closer to the image, and pan across until you can see the area just to the right of the girl's hand. Using the *Paint Bucket* tool, fill the small gap between the girl's glove and the fox on the sign behind.

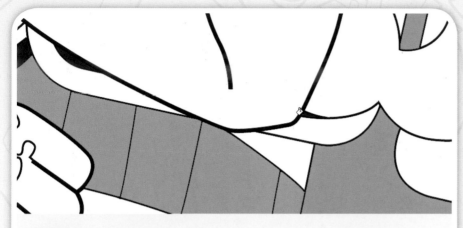

123 There are two more tiny areas of this sign that need filling with color. Zoom in on the bottom of the sign near the girl's elbow. You'll see that there is one small area to fill at either side of her elbow. Use the *Paint Bucket* tool to fill both of these.

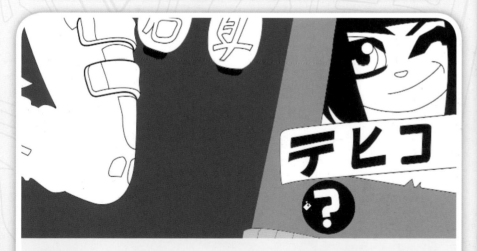

124 Zoom out of the image, then zoom in again on the poster with the girl's face on it at the bottom right of the image. Using the *Paint Bucket* tool with the same dark color selected, click once on the girl's hair to fill it with color.

Next, pan down the image a little and fill each of the three Japanese characters beneath the poster. Note that the first of these is made up of two parts. Finally for this part of the image, pan down a little more and fill the circular area around the question mark with color.

125 Next, zoom out of the image again, and zoom in on the main girl's left arm. We're going to fill the areas of the sign with the letter "g" on it, to the right of her arm.

There are five main areas of this sign outside of the "g" that need filling. Three of these are outside the "g," and two are inside it. Click on them all with the *Paint Bucket* tool to fill them with color.

126 There is still one more small area of the sign to fill. Zoom in close on the curve of the fox's tail, and you will see the gap that still needs color. Click it with the *Paint Bucket* tool to fill it. That's all for this layer for the moment, so save your image using the Ctrl/Cmd+S keyboard shortcut, or by going to *File > Save*.

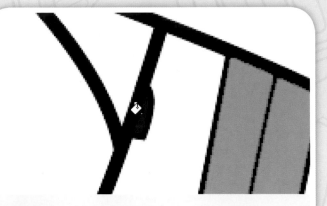

128 There is still one tiny area of Japanese lettering to color on this layer. Zoom in closely on the sign next to the girl's waist, and just below her wrist. You'll see a small section of lettering. Click on this with the *Paint Bucket* tool to fill it with color.

127 For the next coloring section, we'll move back to the Lanterns+Bridge layer. Click on it in the *Layers* palette to select it. Zoom out of the image using the Ctrl/Cmd+O keyboard shortcut, then zoom in again on the Japanese characters beneath the girl's right hand. Click on both of these characters with the *Paint Bucket* tool to fill them with color.

129 Use the Ctrl/Cmd+O keyboard shortcut to zoom all the way out of the image, then zoom in again on the sign with the robin, just above the fire hydrant. There is one sign with Japanese characters to the right of this, and another just above, overlapping it. We'll work on these first.

Click on the three characters on the right-hand sign—the first character has two parts—and fill them all using the *Paint Bucket* tool. Next, fill the background parts of the sign overlapping the robin sign. There are six areas to fill on this sign.

130 Moving on to the bird sign, use the *Paint Bucket* tool to fill the main body of the bird, its wing, both of its legs, and the centers of all of the flowers on the sign.

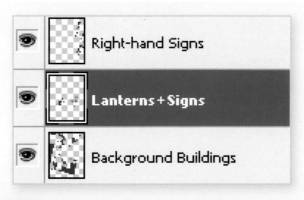

131 Because we added the coloring of the previous signs to the Lanterns+Bridge layer, it makes sense to change the name of the layer so that we remember what's on it. You can change the name of a layer at any time in Photoshop by simply double-clicking on it in the *Layers* palette. Do so now, and rename the layer "Lanterns+Signs."

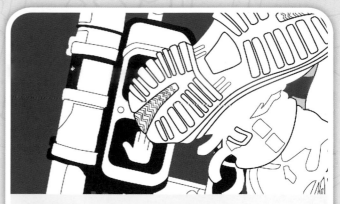

132 Pan up and left across the image until you see the signpost with the Stop sign attached to it. This will be the focus of our next section of coloring.

Stay on our newly renamed Lanterns+Signs layer, and switch to the *Paint Bucket* tool with the same dark purple set as the foreground color. Fill the area of the Stop sign around the hand, then move up and fill the sign directly above it. Next, fill the part on the outer edge of the Stop sign that joins the two signposts together.

133 Next, we'll fill in the shadow areas on the signposts. Start by filling the area above the top bracket on the post, and then the two areas below the second and third brackets.

Move onto the thinner, right-hand post, and fill the area beneath the bracket that holds the bird sign, and the small area beneath the sign with the arrow on.

134 Pan up the image so that you can see the "70" speed sign, and fill the small area directly below it using the *Paint Bucket* tool.

Move over to the larger, left-hand sign, and fill the two shadow areas on the left of this signpost.

135 Zoom in on the joint in the post between the two larger areas that we just filled. Fill the small gaps either side of this joint using the *Paint Bucket* tool.

136 We're now finished with the dark areas of the signs on this side of the image, so zoom out of the image using the Ctrl/Cmd+0 (zero) keyboard shortcut, and zoom in again on the signs with the Japanese characters on at the top-right corner.

Next, click on the Right-hand Signs layer in the *Layers* palette to select it.

137 Switch to the *Paint Bucket* tool and click in the sign to fill it with our dark purple color. Then click in the center of any of the Japanese characters that have gaps in.

When you're done, use the Ctrl/Cmd+0 (zero) keyboard shortcut to zoom all the way out of the image so you can see what we have accomplished so far. We've now finished with the dark, shadowy colors in the background, so save the image using *File > Save*, or Ctrl/Cmd+S.

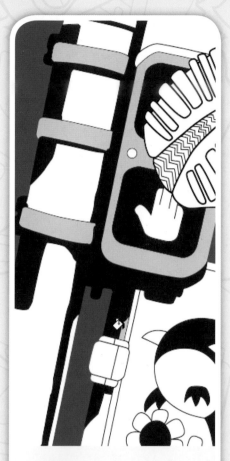

138 We'll now choose a lighter color and start to fill some of the highlight areas on the image. Switch to the *Eyedropper* tool, and pick up the light color that we used on the tops of the curb stones. Zoom in on the curb stones and click on the color with the *Eyedropper* tool to select it.

Zoom out of the image again, then zoom in on the signpost with the Stop sign on it. Click on the Lanterns+Signs layer in the *Layers* palette to select it. The first thing we'll do is fill the brackets on the signpost. Click on the top two brackets with the *Paint Bucket* to fill them with the lighter color.

139 Fill the third bracket with the same light color, then pan right a little to fill the main area of the Stop sign using the *Paint Bucket* tool. Finally, pan down a little and fill the small area above the bracket attaching the bird sign to the thin signpost.

140 There is one more tiny area to fill on the stop sign. Zoom in close where the top part of the sign is covered by the girl's heel. If you look closely, you will see a gap where the tread on the girl's boot heel crosses the light area. Fill this gap with our light color using the *Paint Bucket* tool.

141 Moving back to the post behind the Stop sign, pan down the image slightly and fill the large space below the bracket holding the bird sign.

Next, pan up the signpost and fill the area underneath the arrow sign with our light purple color. Finally, zoom in on the space just above the arrow sign and use the *Paint Bucket* tool to fill this small part of the signpost with color.

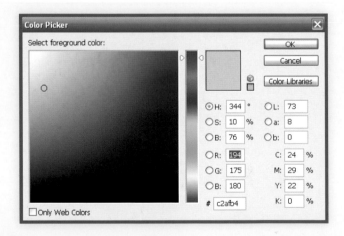

142 We'll now pick a new color to use on the signs. Click on the *Set Foreground Color* button at the bottom of the *Toolbar* to open up the *Color Picker*. Go to the *RGB* fields, and enter R: 170, G: 143, B: 150, then click *OK*. This should give you a slightly darker purple foreground color than we used previously. Don't worry that most of these colors seem quite muted; the colors have been selected to enable the girl to really leap off the background, and to make sure that she is the first thing you see when you look at the image.

143 With the *Paint Bucket* tool selected, click on the sign post above the "70" sign to fill it with our new color. We'll now work our way down the sign post, filling areas as we go. Start by panning down and filling the top of the Stop sign. Pan down a bit more, and fill the small circle at the top-left of the stop sign. Next, pan down a bit farther with the *Hand* tool, and fill the three right-hand segments of the bracket holding the bird sign to the post with color. Finally, pan down to the bottom of the sign and fill the last section with the darker color.

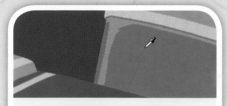

144 We'll use a darker color for some of the other sign areas. Use the Ctrl/Cmd+O (zero) keyboard shortcut to zoom out so that you can see the whole of the image. Switch to the *Eyedropper* tool (or use the Alt/Option key shortcut to temporarily switch to the *Eyedropper*) and click on the dark color that we used at the bottom of the right-hand wall to pick it as the foreground color.

With our new color selected, switch back to the *Paint Bucket* tool, and click on each of the remaining large areas on the left-hand sign post to fill them with the new color.

145 Now that the sign post on the left is finished, we'll move to the thinner post on the right. Zoom in on the bracket holding the bird sign to the post, and fill the remaining three areas with color using the *Paint Bucket* tool.

There are two more areas to fill in with the dark color. First, zoom in on the part of the image where the girl's boot covers the stop sign and fill the hood at the top of the sign. You'll need to zoom in close to fill the gap between the tread in the sole of the boot.

146 Next, zoom out again and pan down to the sign with the bird on. Fill all of the edge parts of the sign using the *Paint Bucket* tool. There should be six separate pieces to click on.

147 Zoom out of the image again, and zoom in on the cat sign in the top-left corner. Fill the top and bottom edges of the sign.

Pan over to the girl's left arm, and zoom in on the area where her arm covers the bridge in the background. Fill the areas of the bridge above and below her arm by clicking on them with the *Paint Bucket* tool.

148 Now, we'll focus on a couple of the signs. Zoom out of the image, then zoom in again on the cat sign at the top left. Switch to the *Eyedropper* tool, and click on the darkest color that we used to shade the left side of the signpost. Switch back to the *Paint Bucket* tool and use this darker color to fill all of the areas of the cat as shown.

Next, pan to the right a little and fill the two numbers on the "70" sign with our dark color.

149 There is one more small area to fill with this dark color. Zoom out of the image, then zoom in on the girl's face. When you can see the face in detail, switch to the *Paint Bucket* tool and fill the area of the girl's glasses that crosses over the fox sign. Now would be a good time to save your image using *File > Save* or the Ctrl/Cmd+S keyboard shortcut.

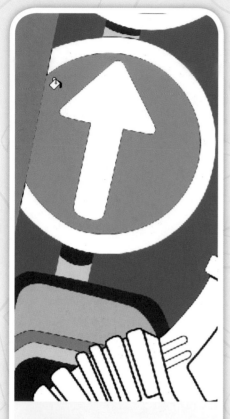

150 It's time to switch to a color other than purple! First, we'll create a new layer on which to store all of the parts filled with this color. Go to the *Layers* palette and click the *Create a New Layer* button. Rename the new layer "Color—Blues."

Click on the *Set Foreground Color* button at the bottom of the *Toolbar* to open the *Color Picker*. Enter R: 85, G: 116, B: 185 into the *Color Picker* and click *OK*. You should now have a mid-blue as your foreground color.

With the Color—Blues layer selected and the *Paint Bucket* tool ready with our new color, zoom in on the arrow sign on the left side of the image and fill the main part of the sign with blue.

151 There are a few other areas we can immediately fill with blue. Pan right from the arrow sign along the line of triangular flags. When you get to the last one next to the girl's head, switch to the *Paint Bucket* tool and fill it with color.

Next, pan right across the girl's head until you reach the first sign with Japanese characters on it. Fill the center part of each of these characters with blue.

152 Pan down the image a little using the *Hand* tool until you can see the fox sign behind the girl's left arm. We'll fill most of the fox's body with blue.

Begin with the fox's head, and fill the two top areas either side of the girl's hand. Then move down a little and fill the small area of the fox's body just above the girl's bicep and the large area to the right by clicking in the tail with the *Paint Bucket* tool. Finally, zoom in close on the fox's face and fill the tiny part of its nose just below the girl's glove.

153 There are a couple more blue areas to fill. First, move down to the poster of the girl's face at the bottom-right of the image. Across the bottom of this poster is a strip of Japanese characters. Click once in the background of this strip with the *Paint Bucket* tool to fill it with blue.

Zoom out of the image so you can see the whole picture on screen, then zoom in again on the bird sign on the left of the image. Fill the entire background of this sign with blue. It should take three clicks with the *Paint Bucket* tool to cover all of the areas around the flowers and the bird.

155 Make sure you are on the Color—Greens layer, then begin by zooming in on the cat sign, and fill the two areas behind the cat's head with our new green color using the *Paint Bucket* tool.

Next, we'll fill a couple of the triangular flags with green. Pan along the image until you can see them clearly, or zoom out and in again, then click on the first and last blank flags with the *Paint Bucket* tool to fill them with green.

154 We've finished with the blues, so now is a good time to save your image using either the *File > Save* command, or the Ctrl/Cmd+S keyboard shortcut.

We're now going to add a new color, and, as before, we'll put this on a new layer. Go to the *Layers* palette and click the *Create a New Layer* button. Double-click on the new layer's name to rename it "Color—Greens."

Click on the *Set Foreground Color* button at the bottom of the *Toolbar* to open the *Color Picker*. Enter R: 172, G: 211, B: 115 and click *OK*. You should now have a pale green as your foreground color.

156 Pan right across the image and fill the edges of the rightmost sign containing Japanese characters with green.

Move down the image from here until you reach the poster with the girl's face on it. Use the *Paint Bucket* tool to fill all of the background areas of this poster with green. There should be five separate areas to fill, including two small areas around the girl's hair. Leave the top corner of the poster that has curled over.

157 Zoom out of the image, then zoom in again on the bird sign at the left of the picture. We'll fill all seven of the petals on the bottom-left flower on this sign with green. You may need to zoom in a bit closer to see them properly, then switch back to the *Paint Bucket* tool to fill them.

Next, move up the image a little until you can see the sign that hangs over the top-right corner of the bird sign. Fill the two main blank areas of this sign with green.

159 This time we'll use a light cyan to fill some of the areas of the image. As before, we'll store all of the areas of this color on a new layer. Click on the *Create a New Layer* button on the *Layers* palette and double-click on the new layer's name to rename it. Call the new layer "Color—Cyans."

Click on the *Set Foreground Color* button at the bottom of the *Toolbar* to bring up the *Color Picker*, then enter R: 152, G: 226, B: 255 and click *OK*. You should now have a cyan set as your foreground color.

158 There are two other areas of this sign that need filling. Zoom in close at the top of the sign, next to the girl's boot, until you can clearly see the two small white gaps. Fill both of these with green using the *Paint Bucket* tool.

Once you've finished, save the image. We're done with the green now, so it's time to start on a new layer.

160 Make sure that you are on the Color—Cyans layers in the *Layers* palette and zoom in on the line of small triangular flags. Switch to the *Paint Bucket* and fill the first blank flag with cyan.

Next, use the *Hand* tool to pan over to the right of the image so you can see the sign containing blue-filled Japanese characters. Fill all of the sections of the outer rim of this sign with cyan. You will need to click in eight different areas—including one that is part of the girl's glasses—to fill the whole shape.

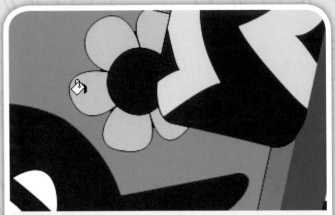

161 For the next area, we'll color some more of the flower petals on the bird sign. Zoom out of the image, then zoom back in on the bird sign at the left. Click on each of the petals of the lower flower with the *Paint Bucket* tool to fill them.

That's the last of the cyan areas, so save your image using the *File > Save* command or the Ctrl/Cmd+S keyboard shortcut.

162 The next color that we use will be orange. Click on the *Create a New Layer* button at the bottom of the *Layers* palette and double-click on the new layer's name to rename it "Color—Oranges."

Click on the *Set Foreground Color* button at the bottom of the *Toolbar* to open the *Color Picker*. Enter R: 247, G: 148, B: 29 into the *Color Picker* and click *OK* to set your foreground color to orange.

Make sure that you are on the Color—Oranges layer and zoom in on the bird sign. Click once on the bird's beak to fill it with orange.

163 We'll now switch to a slightly lighter orange and continue working on this layer. Click on the *Set Foreground Color* button on the *Toolbar* to open the *Color Picker*, and this time enter R: 251, G: 175, B: 93.

Use this new orange color to fill the five petals of the remaining flower on the bird picture.

Pan a little to the right until you can see the small sign with Japanese characters on it directly below the girl's thigh. Fill all of the white gaps on this sign using our new pale orange color. You will have to zoom in to get to the smallest gap at the top of the sign.

164 Zoom out of the image, then zoom in again on the sign with the large blue Japanese characters on the right of the image. We'll fill the outlines of all of these characters with orange. There are eleven areas in all, and some of them are quite small and will require you to zoom in closely to fill them. When you are finished, the sign should be complete.

166 Pan over to the left a little using the *Hand* tool, or the Spacebar keyboard shortcut, until you can see the three signs containing Japanese characters on the bridge behind the girl's right hand. Use the *Paint Bucket* tool to fill each of these signs with orange. Remember to fill the gaps within the characters themselves.

Finally, pan to the right of the image a little until you can see the poster with the girl's face on. Fill the girl's right eye with orange. That's all for the orange areas in the image, so it's a good time to save the file.

165 Zoom out of the image, then zoom in again on the right side of the image where the fox's tail crosses the sign with the "g" on it. Use the *Paint Bucket* to fill the two parts of the letter "g" with our orange color.

167 Click the *Create a New Layer* button in the *Layers* palette, then double-click on the new layer's name and rename it "Color—Reds."

Click on the *Set Foreground Color* button at the bottom of the *Toolbar* to open the *Color Picker*. Enter R: 237, G: 28, B: 36, and click *OK* to set the foreground color to a bright red.

With the Color—Reds layer selected and the *Paint Bucket* tool ready with our new color, zoom out of the image, then zoom in again on the "70" sign at the left of the picture. Fill the outer edge of this sign with red.

169 Next, we'll fill the lanterns with red. Zoom out of the image and zoom in again on the hanging lanterns. Click in the main area of each lantern with the *Paint Bucket* tool to color it red. You will have to zoom in close to the image to fill the smaller gaps within the characters. There should be six areas in all.

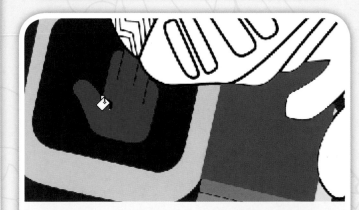

168 Next, pan to the right until you can see the line of triangular flags. Fill the next blank flag along from the left with red.
Pan all the way across to the right of the image and fill all of the Japanese characters in the rightmost sign with red using the *Paint Bucket* tool.

170 Zoom out of the image again, and this time zoom in on the Stop sign. Using the *Paint Bucket* tool, click once on the hand to fill it with our red color.

171 The final part of the image that we'll fill with this color is the fire hydrant. This is quite a complex part of the image, so use the Zoom tool to magnify the image until the fire hydrant fills the screen.

Switch to the *Paint Bucket* tool and start filling areas of the hydrant until your images matches the one shown. There are 24 separate areas to fill. When you have filled all of the areas, save the file.

172 We'll carry on working on the fire hydrant until it's complete. The next task is to pick a darker red to use to fill some more areas. Click on the *Set Foreground Color* button at the bottom of the *Toolbar* to open the *Color Picker*. Enter R: 157, G: 10, B: 14 and click *OK* to set the new foreground color.

Use the *Paint Bucket* tool to fill the hydrant with the new color until your image matches the one shown. There are 44 areas to fill. Again, save your work—you don't want to have to do it all again if your computer crashes!

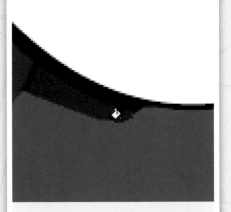

174 The first area to fill is the small white triangle next to the sole of the girl's boot. Zoom in close so you can clearly see the triangle, then click in it with the *Paint Bucket* tool to fill it with red.

Next, pan down to the very tip of the girl's toe, and fill the two areas of the hydrant that are visible below it.

173 We'll now select a darker red to carry on filling the fire hydrant. Open the *Color Picker* by clicking the *Set Foreground Color* button, and enter R: 121, G: 0, B: 0.

Continue using the *Paint Bucket* tool to fill areas with this new darker red. You will need to click 11 times to match the image shown. We'll carry on using this dark color to fill areas, but we'll have to zoom in to work on the smaller parts.

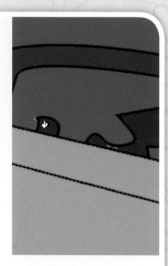

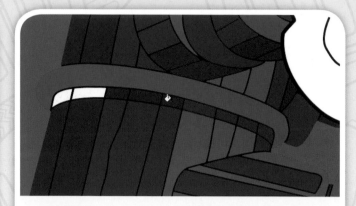

175 Pan down to the nozzle of the hydrant and fill the three remaining blank areas —the two lower sections and the thin vertical line that joins the nozzle to the hydrant arm.

When that's done, move to the bottom of the hydrant and fill the rough areas of cracks and paint chips at its base.

177 Zoom back out a little so you can see the whole hydrant, then switch to the *Paint Bucket* tool. There are five more larger areas of the hydrant to fill with the current dark red color, as shown.

176 You'll notice that there is still a small area on the largest of the paint chips that didn't get filled when we first clicked with the *Paint Bucket*. Zoom in even closer on this area and click in the white or very light gray areas to fill them with red.

178 There should only be four small square pieces of the hydrant left to color. We'll pick an even darker red to fill these.

Click on the *Set Foreground Color* button at the bottom of the *Toolbar* to bring up the *Color Picker*. Enter R: 97, G: 9, B: 10 and click *OK* to set a dark red as the new foreground color. Using the *Paint Bucket* tool, click on the four remaining gaps on the fire hydrant to fill them with red.

That's the fire hydrant, and the reds in the image, finished now, so it's a good time to save the picture.

Right-hand Signs

Color-Yellows

Color-Reds

Color-Oranges

179 Use the Ctrl/Cmd+O (zero) keyboard shortcut to zoom all the way out so you can see the whole of the image at once. The background is really starting to come together now, and there are only a few more colors to add before we can turn our attention to the girl.

Click on the *Create a New Layer* button on the *Layers* palette, then double-click on the name of the new layer. Rename it "Color—Yellows." Click on the *Set Foreground Color* button at the bottom of the *Layers* palette, and enter R: 255, G: 247, B: 153. Then click *OK* to set the foreground color to a pale yellow.

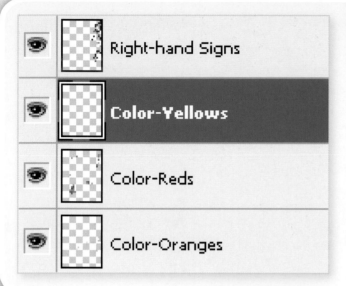

180 Make sure you are on the Color—Yellows layer and zoom and pan around the image to find and fill the following areas with yellow.

The first area is on the cat sign at the far left of the image. Click on both of the cat's eyes with the *Paint Bucket* tool to fill them. Next, move right along the image until you reach the flags next to the girl's head. Fill the two halves of the remaining flag with yellow.

Keep moving right until you reach the girl's left hand. Fill the eye of the fox on the sign behind with yellow. Finally, fill the three curved bridge areas to the right of the girl's head.

181 The next set of yellow areas to fill are quite close by. The first is a small continuation of the bridge line just underneath the girl's chin. The second is another small area just below her armpit.

The next area is another long curve just above the girl's right hand. Finally, pan right to fill the small, triangular area just below the girl's left elbow.

182 There are only a few more yellow areas to fill. The first is the poster of the girl's face on the far right of the image. Fill the main face area, and also the small area left above her eye.

Next, pan down a bit with the *Hand* tool until you can see the question mark. Fill both parts of the question mark with yellow.

The final piece of yellow will be the robin's eye on the far left of the image. Either pan across, or zoom out and zoom back in until you can see the eye clearly, then fill it using the *Paint Bucket*.

Now's a good time to save your work, so go to *File > Save* or press Ctrl/Cmd+S to do so.

183 The next color that we will be using is pink. As usual, we'll create a new layer to hold all of the pink areas.

Click on the *Create a New Layer* button on the *Layers* palette, then double-click on the new layer's name and rename it "Color—Pinks."

Click on the *Set Foreground Color* button on the *Toolbar* to open the *Color Picker*. Enter R: 245, G: 152, B: 157 in the appropriate boxes and click *OK*.

184 Zoom in to the poster of the girl's face at the right of the image. Make sure that you are on the Color—Pinks layer, and fill the girl's nose and the star in her hair with pink using the *Paint Bucket* tool.

Next, pan across to the sign with the robin on at the left of the image. Fill the robin's breast with the same pink color.

185 We'll now pick a slightly lighter pink to color some more areas in the image. Click on the *Set Foreground Color* button on the *Toolbar* to open the *Color Picker*. Enter R: 255, G: 201, B: 204 into the appropriate boxes and click *OK*.

Using the *Hand* tool, pan over to the cat poster on the far left of the image. Switch to the *Paint Bucket* tool, and fill the cat's nose with our new pink color. Zoom out of the image, then zoom back in on the fox sign behind the girl's left hand. Fill the small blank area that's still left between the girl's face and her left hand.

186 That's all of the pink areas complete. Click on the *Create a New Layer* button at the bottom of the *Layers* palette to create the next layer ready for coloring. This layer will solely be used for coloring the cat sign, so double-click on the new layer's name and rename it "Cat Fur."

We'll start with a light brown color, so click on the *Set Foreground Color* button to open the *Color Picker*. Enter R: 165, G: 124, B: 82 into the *Color Picker* and click *OK*.

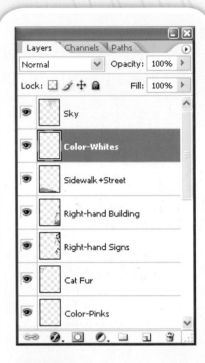

187 Zoom in on the cat sign and switch to the *Paint Bucket* tool. Click on the top section of the cat's fur to fill it with brown, then on the small cheek section on the left side, and the other small fur section at the bottom right.

That's the Cat Fur layer finished with. Save your image by going to *File > Save* or using the Ctrl/Cmd+S keyboard shortcut.

188 Zoom all the way out of the image again by using the Ctrl/Cmd+0 (zero) keyboard shortcut. All of the colors in the background are now complete, but there's still one last thing that we need to do before we move on to coloring the girl. Because we'll be adding special effects to the background, we need to make sure that all of the colors are on their own layers. We've already done this with the colors we've added, but we also need to put the areas that we'll be leaving white on another layer. The simplest way of doing this is by creating a new layer and filling the areas on that layer with white.

Click on the *Create a New Layer* button at the bottom of the *Layers* palette, and double-click on the new layer's name to rename it "Color—Whites." Next, click on the *Set Foreground Color* button at the bottom of the *Toolbar* and enter R: 255, G: 255, B: 255 into the *Color Picker* and click *OK* to choose pure white.

189 We want the whites to sit above the other colors so that they remain crisp against the black lines and other colors below them. To move a layer in the *Layers* palette, you just need to click on it and drag it into its new position. Try it now with the Color—Whites layer. When you click and drag it you'll notice a thick black line that moves between layers in the palette when you move the mouse. This line shows you where the layer will be when you release the mouse. Drag the Color—Whites layer up the stack until it is just below the Sky layer. Don't worry if you make a mistake, you can just click on the layer again and drag it to the correct position.

190 We'll now use a new tool—the *Elliptical Marquee*—to create some circular selections and add highlights to the cat's eyes. For more information on using the *Marquee* tools, see the TIP box opposite. Click on the *Elliptical Marquee* tool in the *Toolbar* and set the selection method in the *Tool Options* bar to *New Selection* (the first button on the bar). Also in the *Tool Options* bar, make sure the *Feather* value is set to O pixels, *Anti-alias* is checked, and the *Style* is set to *Normal*.

Using the *Elliptical Marquee* tool, click on the cat's eye and drag out a small circular shape large enough to fill the area cut out of the pupil. The easiest way to do this is to imagine a rectangle around the ellipse that you are trying to draw. Click the mouse in one of the imaginary corners of the rectangle and drag it to the diametrically opposed corner. You should find that you now have a selection of roughly the right size, but don't worry if it's not in the perfect position. To move the selection, simply click in the middle of it using the same *Marquee* tool and drag it to the correct place. When you're done, go to *Edit > Fill* and choose to fill the selection with the *Foreground Color*.

Once you've finished the first eye, move to the second eye and repeat the process to create a white highlight.

191 Stay on the Color—Whites layer and switch to the *Paint Bucket* tool in the *Toolbar*. Click on each of the main white areas of the cat's face to fill them with color. You might not see a difference, but the layer now contains white shapes exactly the same as those on the cat's face.

TIP The *Marquee* tools are a set of tools used for making regular-shaped selections in Photoshop. They include the *Rectangular Marquee* tool, the *Elliptical Marquee* tool, and two tools for making single-pixel-wide selections. We'll focus on the *Rectangular* and *Elliptical Marquee* tools.

Both tools behave in a similar way—you click and drag a shape around the area that you want to select, and the familiar marching ants appear when you release the mouse to show that a selection has been made. If you hold down the Shift key when you start making a selection, then you will constrain the shape to equal proportions—the *Rectangular Marquee* tool will be constrained to a square, and the *Elliptical Marquee* tool will be constrained to a circle.

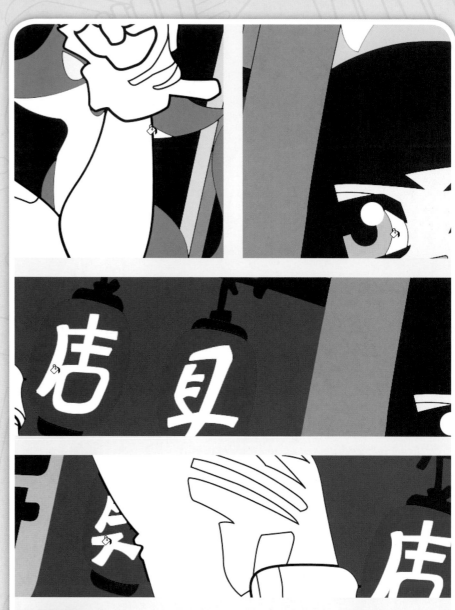

192 We'll carry on filling the white areas in the image. Zoom out, then zoom in again on the speed sign to the right of the cat. Fill the main background of the sign and the hole in the "O" with white using the *Paint Bucket* tool.

Next, pan down a little and fill the outer edge of the arrow sign and the arrow itself with white.

193 Zoom out of the image again, and zoom in on the fox sign behind the girl's left arm. Fill both of the blank areas of the fox with white.

We'll tidy up the rest of the image now, too. Pan down to the poster with the girl's face on it and fill the three blank areas of the poster with white (the corner of the poster and the two white parts of the girl's eye). Finally, fill in all of the Japanese characters on the hanging lanterns. There are two on the right side of the girl, and one—made up of two parts—on the left side of the girl.

194 Zoom out to view the whole image by using the Ctrl/Cmd+0 (zero) keyboard shortcut. The background is now completely colored. We still need to add some special effects to it, but we'll do that when the girl image is completed. For now, save the background using Ctrl/Cmd+S, and go to *File > Close* to close the image.

195 We're now going to start coloring the separate image of the girl. Download the Manga_Girl.tif file from the website address on the front cover flap. Alternatively, you can scan in the image on page 96 of this book. Scan it as black and white and at 600 pixels per inch (PPI), and name it Manga_Girl.tif. When you have saved the image onto your computer, open it in Photoshop.

The first thing that we'll do is convert the image to RGB. This means that we can apply color to the image. Go to *Image > Mode > RGB Color*.

Next, save the image as a PSD file. We do this because, as we discussed earlier, PSD is Photoshop's standard file format and supports all of Photoshop's abilities such as layers.

196 Now that the file is set up correctly, we can start working on it. First, we need to convert the Background layer of the image into a normal layer. The Background layer is a special layer that cannot have certain effects, such as transparency, applied to it. To change it, all we need to do is rename the layer. Double-click on the Background layer's name and rename it "Girl Lines 1."

197 We're now going to separate the girl from the background. The easiest way to do this is by using the *Magic Wand* tool. Switch to the *Magic Wand* tool in the *Toolbar* and check the settings in the *Tool Options* bar—they should read *Tolerance*: 32, *Anti-alias*: checked, *Contiguous*: checked, *Sample All Layers*: checked. Make sure you choose *Add to Selection* mode.

Click on the large area of background to start the selection. This will get most of the background in one click, but there are a couple of missing areas. First, click in the area between the girl's right foot and her arm. Next, click in the smaller area between her face and the frame of her glasses. Finally, zoom in next to her right ear and you will see a small triangular gap between two strands of her hair. Click in this gap to add it to the selection.

With the selection complete, press the Backspace key on your keyboard to remove the white background from the image (the checkerboard pattern in Photoshop shows that there's nothing there).

198 Go to *Select > Inverse*. This will select the opposite of your previous selection, so you will have the girl selected rather than the background.

We're doing this because we want to fill the girl with a single color first, and then build up more colors on top of that base. Click the *Create a New Layer* button at the bottom of the *Layers* palette, double-click on the new layer's name, and rename it "Color—Flesh 1."

Click on the *Set Foreground Color* button at the bottom of the *Toolbar* to open the *Color Picker*. Enter R: 210, G: 153, B: 129 and click *OK* to set a dark pink skin tone as your foreground color.

199 We'll now fill the selection with our skin color. Go to *Edit > Fill*, and make sure that *Use* is set to *Foreground Color*. When you're done, press Ctrl/Cmd+D on the keyboard to deselect the selection.

The lines in the image have been completely covered by the skin color, so we need to find a way of making them stand out above it. First, make a copy of the Girl Lines 1 layer. Click on the layer in the *Layers* palette then go to *Layer > Duplicate Layer*, then click *OK* to accept the default layer name.

Next, we need to put the duplicate layer above the Color—Flesh 1 layer. Click on the Girl Lines 1 Copy layer in the *Layers* palette and drag it above the Color—Flesh 1 layer. The lines are now above the skin color, but we can't see the skin color any more!

200 The answer is to change the blending mode of the layer. Blending modes affect how a layer blends with the layers beneath it. The blending mode is set from the drop-down menu at the top of the *Layers* palette, which usually reads *Normal*.

Make sure you are on the Girl Lines 1 Copy layer, and click on the blending modes drop-down menu. We'll use *Multiply* mode here, which effectively means that the white parts of the layer will become invisible, leaving just the black lines. When you click on *Multiply*, you should see the image change so that the girl is flesh-colored, but the black lines are still visible.

201 We'll now pick a new color and start adding some darker skin tones to make the girl look more three-dimensional.

Click on the *Create a New Layer* button at the bottom of the *Layers* palette, then double-click on the new layer's name and rename it "Color—Flesh 2."

Click on the *Set Foreground Color* button at the bottom of the *Toolbar* to open the *Color Picker,* and enter R: 147, G: 91, B: 82. Click *OK*.

202 Zoom in on the girl's face. We'll now start filling the girl's features with our new, darker flesh color.

Make sure that you are working on the Color—Flesh 2 layer and select the *Paint Bucket* tool from the *Toolbar*. Start by filling the smaller areas around her ear, then carry on across the face and onto her neck until you have filled all of the areas of her face as shown.

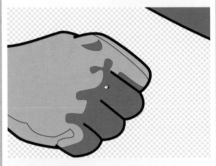

203 Pan right a little across the image until you can see the girl's left arm. Fill the underside of her thumb and then the knuckle of each of her fingers. Finally, click on the large area of her arm to fill that, too.

Next, move down the image a little until you can see her other arm, and fill the front part of her fist and two smaller areas on her first finger.

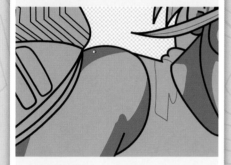

205 Next, we'll add some highlights to the girl by using some lighter flesh tones. As usual, we'll do this on a new layer.

Click on the *Create a New Layer* button in the *Layers* palette, and rename the layer "Color—Flash 3."

Click on the *Set Foreground Color* button at the bottom of the *Toolbar* to open the *Color Picker*. Enter R: 234, G: 188, B: 168 into the *Color Picker* and click *OK* to set a lighter pink as the foreground color.

204 We'll now carry on filling areas of the girl's right arm.

First, fill the two areas on the underside of her wrist and forearm. Then carry on up the arm and fill the two areas either side of her bicep.

Next, move to the top of her arm and fill the small area on her shoulder. That's all of the darker areas of skin finished with. Now would be a good time to save your file.

206 Zoom out of the image, then zoom back in on the girl's face. We'll begin by coloring some of the areas on the right of her face. Begin by filling the rightmost part of her forehead using the *Paint Bucket* tool, and then carry on down her face until you have colored all of the areas shown. There are a few small areas around her eye and her nose, so you may need to zoom in a bit closer.

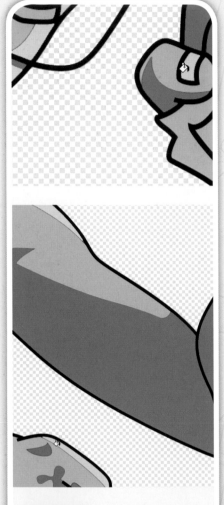

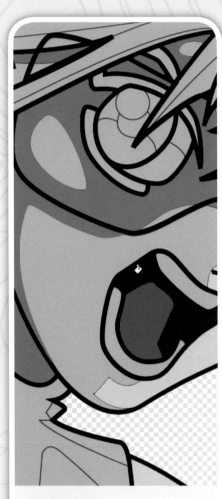

207 Switch to the *Hand* tool, or use the Spacebar keyboard shortcut, to pan across the image over to the girl's left arm. Click on her thumbnail with the *Paint Bucket* tool to fill it with the lighter pink.

Pan a little farther down her arm and fill the small area at the top of her shoulder and the thin horizontal strip at the top of her right hand.

208 We'll now pick a new color to fill the area inside the girl's mouth. First, create a new layer by clicking the *Create a New Layer* button on the *Layers* palette. Double-click on the new layer's name and rename it "Color—Mouth." Click on the *Set Foreground Color* button on the *Toolbar* to open the *Color Picker*, and enter R: 146, G: 61, B: 73. Click *OK*. This will give you a dark pink foreground color.

Switch to the *Paint Bucket* tool and click on the lower area inside the girl's mouth to fill it with our new color.

209 Next, we'll pick a new color for the remaining area of her mouth. Click on the *Set Foreground Color* button again to open the *Color Picker* and enter R: 62, G: 26, B: 31 then click *OK*. Still on the Color— Mouth layer, click on the top section of the mouth to fill it with the new darker color.

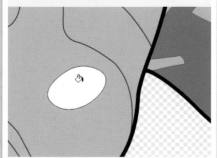

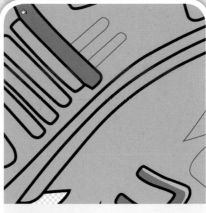

210

We can quickly finish off the mouth area by coloring the girl's teeth. We'll do this in a new layer, as there are a few other areas we can fill with white at the same time.

Click on the *Create a New Layer* button at the bottom of the *Layers* palette, then rename the new layer "Color—Whites." Click on the *Set Foreground Color* button on the *Toolbar* to open the *Color Picker* and enter R: 255, G: 255, B: 255 to set the foreground color to pure white.

Using the *Paint Bucket* tool on the Color—Whites layer, click on her two rows of teeth to fill them with white. Next, pan up the image and fill the four highlight areas of the girl's eyes as shown.

Finally, pan down the image and fill the small circular area on the front of the girl's vest.

211

There are a few areas of gray color that we'll also put on the Color—Whites layer. Click on the *Set Foreground Color* button to open the *Color Picker*, then enter R: 172, G: 172, B: 172 to select a light gray. Pure grays are always an equal mix of all three primary colors.

Zoom out of the image and zoom back in on the girl's face. Click on the two top-right areas of her glasses to fill them with color.

There are two more small areas to fill, but they're spread over the image. Zoom out, then zoom in again on the girl's belt buckle and fill the three small highlights on the buckle. Lastly, zoom out and zoom in again on the buckle on her kicking boot. Fill the highlight on this buckle.

212

We'll carry on filling these buckles with a darker gray. Bring up the *Color Picker* by clicking on the *Set Foreground Color* button on the *Toolbar* and enter R: 101, G: 101, B: 101 to get a dark gray foreground color.

Fill the remainder of her boot buckle with the dark gray. Next, pan to the left so that you can see her boot and fill the long bar at the top of her boot heel with gray.

Zoom out and zoom in again on the girl's belt. Fill the three remaining areas of her belt buckle, then also fill the thin top section on either side of her belt.

Lastly, zoom out and in again on her other boot and fill both parts of the buckle there with the dark gray color.

213 We're now going to color the girl's hair. As with her body, we'll first select it all, fill it with a base color, and then add shadows and highlights to give it shape.

Switch to the *Magic Wand* tool set to *Add to Selection* mode and start clicking on every part of the girl's hair. It's quite a complex job, but it shouldn't take too long. Remember to make use of the *Quick Mask* to check which areas you've selected and which are still to be done. Turn the *Quick Mask* on by clicking the *Edit in Quick Mask Mode* button at the bottom of the *Toolbar*, or by pressing Q on the keyboard. To return to making selections, Click on the *Edit in Standard Mode* button, or press Q again. If you're ever unsure whether an area has been selected or not, click on it again with the *Magic Wand* tool; it doesn't matter if you click on an area twice.

There are a few small areas of hair, especially around her glasses, but in general, all of the pieces to select are quite large. If you ever click on the black lines by mistake, just press Ctrl/Cmd+Z on the keyboard to undo.

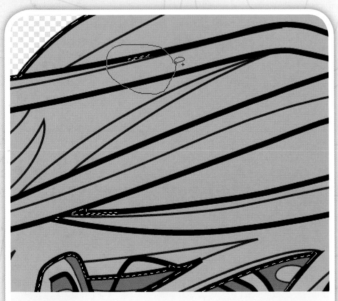

214 The current selection area still has a few tiny gaps in it that will show up when we fill it with color. To fix this, go to *Select > Modify > Expand*, and enter a value of 5 pixels in the box that appears. This should add most of the lines in the hair to the selection, but there are still a few small unselected spots within the hair.

Switch to the *Lasso* tool—it's next to the *Magic Wand* tool—and make sure that it is set to *Add to Selection* in the *Tool Options* bar. Then just draw rough circles around each of the unselected areas to add them to the selection.

215 Click on the Color—Flesh 1 layer in the *Layers* palette, then go to *Layer > New > Layer via Copy*. Rename the new layer as "Color—Hair."

We'll now select a color for the girl's hair. Open the *Color Picker* and enter R: 121, G: 0, B: 38 to set a dark red as the foreground color. You'll notice that the girl's hair was deselected when we created the new layer, but don't worry, you don't have to go through and select it all over again. Simply Ctrl/Cmd+click on the Color—Hair layer's thumbnail in the *Layers* palette and a selection of the entire contents of the layer will be generated.

Now, go to *Edit > Fill* and choose *Use: Foreground Color*, then click *OK*. The girl's hair will now be colored dark red. Use the Ctrl/Cmd+D keyboard shortcut to deselect the selection, and save the image with Ctrl/Cmd+S when you're done.

216 Create a new layer and rename it "Color—Hair 2." We'll use this layer for adding a brighter color to the girl's hair. Open the *Color Picker* and enter R: 157, G: 0, B: 57 to give you a more magenta color for the foreground.

Use the *Magic Wand* to select the areas shown, then use *Edit > Fill* to fill them with our new foreground color. Press Ctrl/Cmd+D to deselect the selection when you're done.

217 For the final color on her hair we'll use an even lighter magenta. Remain on the Color—Hair 2 layer and open the *Color Picker*. Enter R: 237, G: 20, B: 90 and click *OK* to set a bright magenta as the foreground color.

Again, use the *Magic Wand* tool to select the areas as shown, and then *Edit > Fill* to fill them with our new foreground color. Deselect the selection when you've finished by pressing Ctrl/Cmd+D.

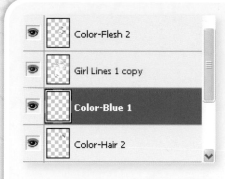

218 We've completed the girl's hair, so we'll create a new layer to start applying another new color.

Click on the *Create a New Layer* button in the *Layers* palette and rename it "Color—Blue 1." Open the *Color Picker* and enter R: 0, G: 54, B: 99, then click *OK* to set the foreground color to a dark blue.

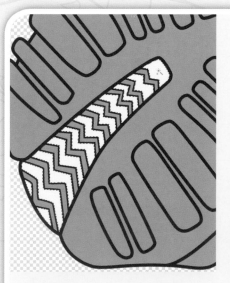

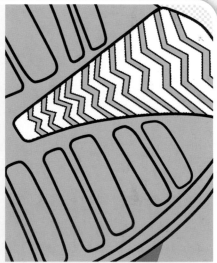

219 Zoom in on the sole of the girl's boot. We'll make a selection of the blue areas of the image, starting with the two zigzag tread sections of the sole. Zoom in close to the bottom section and switch to the *Magic Wand* tool. Start with the highest section of tread, and click on alternate zigzag sections to add them to the selection. You will have to click twice to get the last section.

Pan up to the top section of tread and do the same. Start by clicking on the highest piece and click on alternate zigzag sections until you reach the end.

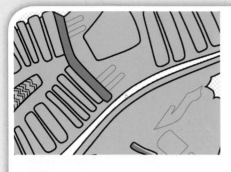

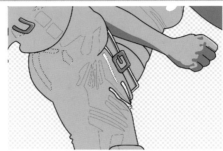

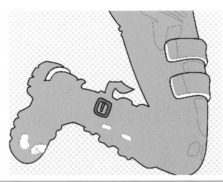

220 Zoom out a little and click on the edge of the sole of the girl's boot with the *Magic Wand* tool to add it to the selection.

Next, zoom out a little farther and start adding the small areas along her leg to the selection, as shown. Use the Spacebar keyboard shortcut to temporarily switch to the *Hand* tool and pan down her leg a little more. Switch back to the *Magic Wand* and continue adding areas to the selection as shown. You may need to zoom in closer to accurately select parts of her belt.

Finally, continue down her leg and add the two areas on her thigh pads, a couple of small areas on her shin, and then three areas on her boot.

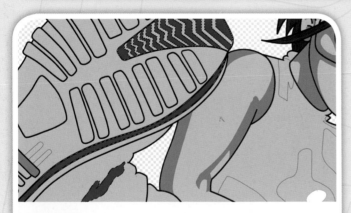

221 Just as with her hair, we'll expand this selection a little to fill any small gaps and to help hide some of the lines. Go to *Select > Modify > Expand*, and enter a value of 3 pixels.

With that done, we can fill the selection with our blue color. Go to *Edit > Fill* and choose *Foreground Color* to fill with. Press Ctrl/Cmd+D to deselect the selection, then Ctrl/Cmd+S to save the image so far.

222 We're going to color the girl's eyes blue. Zoom out of the image and zoom in on her face.

Using the *Magic Wand* tool, select the upper areas of both of her eyes. You will have to click five times to complete the selection. As before, we'll expand the selection a little before filling it. Go to *Select > Modify > Expand* and enter a value of 1 pixel in the box that appears, then click *OK*.

Finally, go to *Edit > Fill* to fill the selection with the foreground blue color, then press Ctrl/Cmd+D to deselect the selection.

223

There is one final area of dark blue to fill. Pan across to the right slightly until you can see the girl's clenched fist. Click once with the *Magic Wand* tool in the palm of her glove, then again on the first part of the glove, at the base of her fingers.

Go to *Select > Modify > Expand* to expand the selection and enter a value of 3 pixels. When this is done, go to *Edit > Fill* to fill the selection with blue, then press Ctrl/Cmd+D to deselect.

That's the dark blue finished with, so create a new layer for our next color and rename it "Color—Blue 2." Open the *Color Picker* and enter R: 0, G: 74, B: 128 and click *OK* to set the foreground color to a slightly lighter blue.

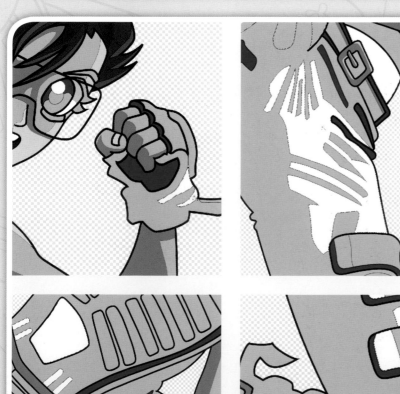

224

The first two areas to select for our new color can be found on the same glove as we have just been working on. Click on the two large triangular areas directly below the girl's palm to begin the selection.

Next, move over to her right leg. Click on the large area on her thigh to add it to the selection, then add the two square areas on her boot, the four small rectangular areas just above the heel on her sole, and the central section of the sole.

Now zoom out of the image and zoom in again on the girl's left leg. Click on all of the large areas at the top of her thigh with the *Magic Wand* tool to add them to the selection. Also, click on the area of her midriff just above her belt.

Carry on down her thigh and add the two areas on the left of her thigh pads, the two areas between the pads, and the two smaller areas on her knee.

225 Go to *Select > Modify > Expand* and expand this selection by 3 pixels. Then go to *Edit > Fill* and fill it with our new foreground color. Deselect the selection using Ctrl/Cmd+D.

We'll now create a new layer for our next color. Create a new layer in the *Layers* palette and rename it "Color—Blue 3."

Click on the *Set Foreground Color* button in the *Toolbar* to open the *Color Picker* and enter R: 0, G: 118, B: 163 to choose a lighter blue color.

We will be coloring the majority of the girl's costume in black, so these similarly toned blue colors will stand out well against that, and against the colors that we picked for the background.

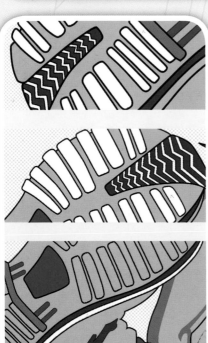

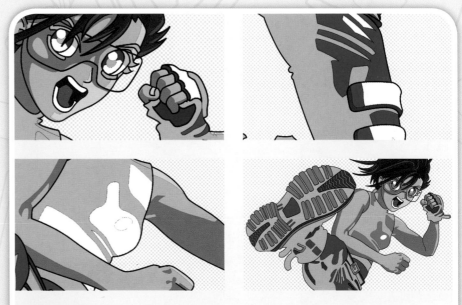

226 We'll start the new color by filling the rest of her boot tread. Zoom in close on her boot and begin by selecting all of the remaining zigzag areas of the tread. Next, click on all of the oblong areas of tread on either side of her sole to add them to the selection. When you're done, click on the top section of her sole, next to her boot, to add that to the selection also.

227 Continuing with the same selection, pan over to the girl's face and click on the two lower areas of the girl's eyes with the *Magic Wand* tool to add them to the selection. Moving slightly to the right, add the top part of her glove to the selection, and the small area that sticks out on the far right of the glove.

Next, pan down to the girl's vest and add all of the main areas with outlines around them. There should be six areas, including the small triangular section under her arm.

Lastly, pan down to her leg and select the two highlight areas at the top of her thigh, and the two large areas of her thigh pads.

As before, we'll now expand the selection slightly before filling it. Go to *Select > Modify > Expand* and enter a value of 3 pixels into the box that appears, then click *OK*. Go to *Edit > Fill*, selecting *Foreground Color*, to fill the selection with our light blue. Deselect the selection. If you zoom out of the image now, you'll see the girl is really beginning to take shape. We'll add one more layer of bright blue highlights before we fill the main parts of her costume with black.

228

Create a new layer and name it "Color—Blue 4." Click on the *Set Foreground Color* button to open the *Color Picker*, and enter R: 0, G: 173, B: 239 to choose a bright blue color.

Zoom in on the girl's arm and glove. There are only two areas that we'll color with this bright blue. The first is the far-right part of her glove, and the second is the shoulder part of her vest—you will have to click twice with the *Magic Wand* tool to select this area.

When you're done, go to *Select > Modify > Expand* and enter 3 pixels into the box. Fill the selection with the foreground blue color by going to *Edit > Fill*, then deselect the selection by pressing Ctrl/Cmd+D.

229

Before we move onto the black areas of the image, we'll need to re-order our layers slightly. This is because some of the most recent blue areas that we added are overlapping the first blue areas that we made. This is most apparent on the girl's eyes.

Zoom in on the eyes and you will see a thin line of light blue encroaching on the area of dark blue. We can fix this by moving the layer containing the dark blue to a position above the light blue layer in the *Layers* palette.

Click on the Color—Blue 1 layer in the *Layers* palette and drag it up above the Color—Blue 4 layer. When you release the mouse button, the layer should be in its correct position, and the light blue color should no longer cross over into the dark blue.

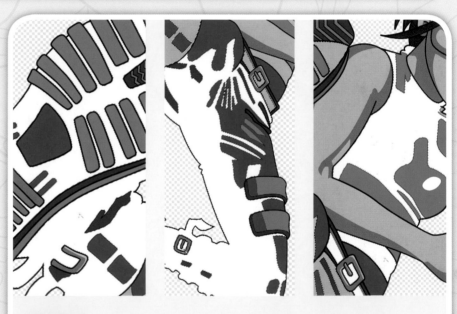

230

We're now ready to color the rest of the girl with black. First, create a new layer and rename it "Color—Black." This layer should now be above Color—Blue 1 in the *Layers* palette. We now need to click in all of the remaining areas of the girl's clothing to select them, then we'll fill them all with black.

Start by clicking once on the sole of her boot with the *Magic Wand* tool to select it all, then make your way down her boot and onto her legs. You should only need to click once on her boot, and once on her leg, to select the majority of these areas, but you will also need to zoom in a little farther to select three smaller areas on her legs—the lower buckle on her boot, the square area just above her thigh pads, and one of the thin creases at the top of her thigh.

Next, select the three areas of her belt and the part of her vest just above it. Pan up a little and click once on her vest to select it, then once more on the small part of her collar that's not yet selected. Finally, click once on her glove to add it to the selection.

231 That's all of her clothing selected now, but we'll also color her eyelashes and eyebrows black.

Zoom in on the girl's face so that you can see her eyes. Click on each of the areas of her eyelashes and eyebrows with the *Magic Wand* tool to add them to the selection. You may need to zoom in even closer to select the final small areas where her glasses cross her eyelashes. Click once in each of her pupils to add those to the selection, too.

Once the selection is complete, go to *Select > Modify > Expand* and enter a value of 3 pixels into the box. Now we need to set our foreground color to black. You can either open the *Color Picker* and set all three RGB fields to 0, or press D on the keyboard to reset the foreground and background colors to black and white. Go to *Edit > Fill* and fill the selection with our foreground color, black. Deselect the selection when you're done.

232 Before moving on, make sure that there are no uncolored areas that should be black. This is especially likely in her eyes, so zoom in close on that area to take a look. If there are any small areas of flesh color left, as shown above, then they need to be filled with black.

The easiest way of filling them is to switch to the *Lasso* tool in the *Toolbar* and draw a small circle around the area to create a selection. Then just go to *Edit > Fill* to fill the small selection with black. Fill any other flesh-colored spots that you see in the same way.

Zoom out of the image using the Ctrl/Cmd+0 (zero) shortcut so that you can see the complete image. You will see that the girl is almost finished.

There are two final things that we need to do to the image before we combine the girl image with the background image. The first is to add a couple more highlights to the eyes, and the second is to do all of the coloring on her glasses.

Before we do the final bits of tidying up, we will merge all of the layers in the image together. We do this to make it easy to transfer the girl across to our background image.

Go to *Layer > Merge Visible* to merge all of the layers together. The main image will look the same, but you'll notice that there is now only one layer in the *Layers* palette. The layers are merged into the one layer that was selected, so in our case it's the Color—Black layer. Double-click on this layer's name to rename it "Girl Layer."

233

Now to add the highlights to the eyes. Create a new layer, then rename it "Eye Glow."

We'll create these new highlights in the same way that we did the white highlights. Switch to the *Elliptical Marquee* tool at the top left of the *Toolbar* and make sure that it is set to *Add to Selection* mode in the *Tool Options* bar. Zoom in on the area around the girl's eyes so that you can clearly see what you're doing, and click the mouse to the left of her first pupil. After you click, hold down the Shift key and drag to create a small circular selection as shown. Remember that holding the Shift key constrains the shape to a perfect circle. Drag three more circles out in the same way until you have an arrangement similar to that shown.

Click on the *Set Foreground Color* button to open the *Color Picker* and enter R: 109, G: 207, B: 246 to choose a light blue color. Go to *Edit > Fill* to fill the highlights with our new blue color. Deselect the selection by pressing Ctrl/Cmd+D.

Finally, we need to blend the new highlights with the rest of the eye. The easiest way to do this is to set the blending mode of the layer. Remember that this is controlled by the drop-down box at the top of the *Layers* palette. Click on this box and select *Overlay*.

234

Now, on to the girl's glasses. We want them to look shiny and to glow a little, so we'll spend some time on getting the effect right.

First, create a new layer called "Sunglasses" at the top of the *Layers* palette. We now need to make a selection enclosing all of her sunglasses except for the areas where her hair crosses over them. The easiest way to do this is by using the *Polygonal Lasso* tool. We haven't used this tool before, but you'll find it underneath the *Lasso* tool in the *Toolbar*. Hold the mouse button down on the *Lasso* tool icon until a pop-up menu appears, and select the *Polygonal Lasso* tool.

The *Polygonal Lasso* tool behaves in the same way as the *Lasso* tool, but instead of making freehand selections, it makes selections using straight lines. Start with the top-left area of her glasses. Click once in the middle of the black line where her hair crosses her glasses. You'll notice now that when you move the mouse, a thin straight line runs between your cursor and the first place that you clicked. Move farther along the black line around her glasses and click again. Now when you move the mouse, the line goes between the last point and the cursor. Continue around the triangle of her glasses that's crossed by her hair—trying to keep in roughly the middle of the black line—until you get back to where you started.

If you look closely at the cursor when you hold it over the original start position, you'll notice that there is a small circle next to the cursor. This means that when you click, the selection will be complete and the marching ants will appear.

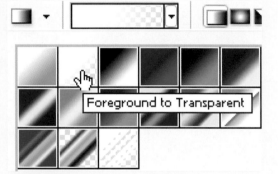

Foreground to Transparent

235 Still using the *Polygonal Lasso* tool, click on *Add to Selection* mode in the *Tool Options* bar, then click on part of the line in the main part of the glasses and work your way around the shape as before. Take your time going around the shape, especially around the corners and the places where her hair crosses the glasses, until you end up back where you started and complete the selection. If you need to, you can still pan around the image by holding the Spacebar to temporarily switch to the *Hand* tool. It will switch back to the *Polygonal Lasso* tool with your selection unaffected when you release the key.

You should now have a complete selection of the area covered by the girl's sunglasses. With that done, it's time to color them. Open the *Color Picker* and select R: 0, G: 166, B: 80 to choose a solid green color. Go to *Edit > Fill* to fill the selection with our new foreground color. Deselect the selection.

236 Obviously, we can't leave the glasses looking like that! Click on the *Blending Mode* drop-down menu at the top of the *Layers* palette and change the layer to *Soft Light* mode. This means that the green glasses will show the correct tints of the colors beneath.

Create a new layer and name it "Shine 1." We'll use this layer to add some highlights to the glasses to look like light reflecting in them. We'll create this effect with a gradient. First of all, set the foreground color to white by opening the *Color Picker* and entering R: 255, G: 255, B: 255.

Select the *Gradient* tool from the *Toolbar*. This is underneath the *Paint Bucket* tool, so click and hold the cursor over the *Paint Bucket* icon until the fly-out menu appears, then select the *Gradient* tool.

There are a couple of things that we need to set in the *Tool Options* bar before we use the tool. First, click on the *Linear Gradient* button—the first of the five gradient types. Next, click on the first drop-down menu (with the gradient color in it) and select the *Foreground to Transparent* gradient. This means that the gradient will start with white, then gradually fade out to nothing.

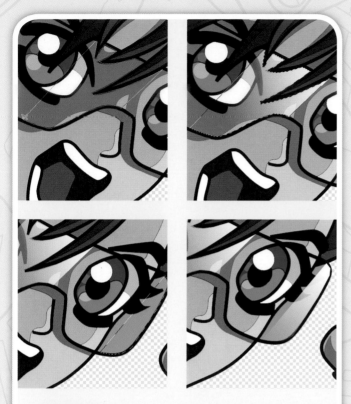

237 Before we apply the gradient tool, we need to select an area for it to fill. Switch to the *Polygonal Lasso* tool and make a selection around an area of the glasses similar to that shown. Don't worry if you cross over the black lines—you won't be able to see this when we change the blending mode of the layer later.

When the selection is complete, switch back to the *Gradient* tool. Click in the top right of the selection, drag down to the bottom left of the selection, and release the mouse. You should see a gradient appear inside the selection area. Deselect the selection.

We'll now repeat the process to create a similar highlight on the right side of the glasses. Switch to the *Polygonal Lasso* tool and make a selection area similar to the one shown. Switch to the *Gradient* tool and again, drag a gradient from the top right of the selection down to the bottom left, then deselect the selection.

238 The highlights are too intense, so we'll change the blending mode of the Shine 1 layer to *Overlay*.

We'll now create a soft glow around the highlights. Duplicate the Shine 1 layer by going to *Layer > Duplicate Layer* and rename the new layer "Shine 2."

This layer is going to be blurred to create the glow effect. We can easily achieve this by using one of Photoshop's filters. Photoshop has many filters—we'll use a few more later—but one of the simplest things you can do is blur an image. Go to *Filter > Blur > Gaussian Blur*. Enter *Radius*: 6 in the box that appears, then click *OK* to apply the filter. You should now see a soft glow around the highlights.

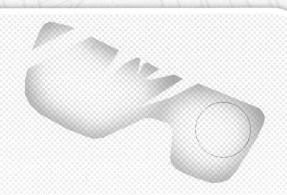

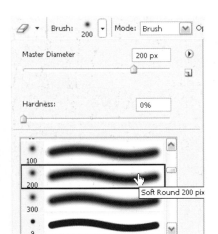

239 Next, duplicate the Sunglasses layer by clicking on it in the *Layers* palette and then going to *Layer > Duplicate Layer*. Rename the layer "Shine 3."

We now want to hide all of the other layers so that we just see our new layer. Right/Ctrl+click on the eye icon next to the layer's thumbnail and then select *Show/Hide All Other Layers*.

We'll use this layer to create a glow around the edge of the glasses. We'll achieve this by erasing the inner parts of the glasses on this layer, leaving a thin band around the outside.

Switch to the *Eraser* tool (situated next to the *Paint Bucket* tool in the *Toolbar*) and move to the *Tool Options* bar. Click on the *Brush* drop-down menu and select a *Soft Round 200 Pixels* brush. Place the large round cursor over the areas shown and click to erase most of the inner parts of the glasses.

When you're done, Right/Ctrl+click on the eye icon next to the layer in the *Layers* palette and select *Show/Hide All Other Layers* to show the other layers.

240 The girl is completely finished now, so zoom out to reveal the whole image to see her in all her glory.

Before we transfer her across to the background, we should tidy up the *Layers* palette. We want to keep the sunglasses effects separate from the rest of the image, so we'll put them into a layer group. Layer groups are a convenient way of organizing your layers—see the TIP box for more information.

Click on the *Create a New Group* button at the bottom of the *Layers* palette and double-click on its name to rename it—call it "Girl Effects." Click on the top layer in the *Layers* palette (it should be Shine 2) then Ctrl/Cmd+click on the rest of the effects layers to select them all. Note that you should click on the layer's name, not the thumbnail. When they are all selected, click and drag them over the layer group and release the mouse button to move them into the group folder. Click on the arrow next to the group's icon in the *Layers* palette to collapse the group.

Create another group in the same way, and rename this one "Girl." Select both Girl Layer and the Girl Effects group and drag them into the new Girl group. Again, click on the small arrow next to the group to collapse it and hide the layers.

241 Now it's time to copy the girl across to the background. First, save the girl image by going to *File > Save*. Next, open the Manga_Art.psd file that contains the colored background. Don't close the girl image when you do this—we'll need them both open at once.

Before we add the two images together, let's tidy up the layers in the background image to make it easier to deal with. There aren't any effects in this layer, so we can just merge all of the layers together. The simplest way of doing this is to flatten the layer. Working on the Manga_Art image file, go to *Layer > Flatten Image*. You'll see that all that's left in the *Layers* palette is a single Background layer.

242 Let's put our two images together. Go to *Window Arrange > Tile Vertically* so that you can see both images at the same time. Switch to the *Move* tool (the black arrow icon at the top of the *Toolbar*) and click on the girl image to select it.

Next, click on the girl, drag her across onto the background image, and release the mouse button. You may need to make sure that the Girl layer group is selected before you can drag the girl.

Don't worry about positioning the girl yet. First, go back to the girl image and go to *File > Close* to close it. Resize the remaining window so that you can see the whole image on the screen, then use the *Move* tool to drag the girl into position. If you find it difficult to position her precisely with the mouse, you can use the cursor (arrow) keys on the keyboard to move the girl into exactly the right place.

When she's in the correct position, go to *File > Save* to save the image.

TIP Layer groups are very similar to the folders that you use to store your files on your computer. You can keep all of the layers that you're not using tucked away in a layer group, and then only reveal the content of the group when you need to work on it. This means that you don't end up scrolling through hundreds of layers in your *Layers* palette trying to find the correct layer to work on.

243 Before we start adding more effects, we need to clean up the image a little. If you zoom in closely on the edges of the girl, you'll notice that there is a fine white line surrounding her. This is left over from when we originally extracted the girl from the white background.

Click on the arrow next to the Girl group to open it, then click on Girl Layer to select it. Ctrl/Cmd+click on the layer's thumbnail to generate a selection from the content of the layer. You'll see the familiar marching ants appear around the girl. We want to remove some of the pixels from the edges of the girl. The easiest way to do this is to select everything except the girl, enlarge the selection slightly, and then delete it.

Go to *Select > Inverse* to select the blank space on the Girl Layer. Next, go to *Select > Modify > Expand* and expand the selection by 2 pixels. We'll also apply a feather to this selection. Feathering a selection is similar to blurring its outline, and will help avoid any harsh lines around the selection edge. Go to *Select > Feather* and enter a *Feather Radius* of 2 pixels. When you're done, press the Backspace key on the keyboard to delete the selected area, and then deselect the selection. The white line should have disappeared.

244 Now it's time to start adding the special effects. Photoshop is a hugely versatile program, and there are literally millions of different effects that you could add. If you want to, you can save a copy of this stage of the file by going to *File > Save As* and saving the image under a different name. You can then come back to the image when you've got a bit more confidence and apply some wild effects of your own!

For now, though, follow the rest of the steps here to give you an idea of what's possible. Click the arrow next the Girl group again to collapse the group, then click on Girl Layer to select it. Switch to the *Magic Wand* tool and click on the orange part of the letter "g" on the right. We need to select all of the orange parts of the layer, but don't worry—you don't need to click on them all individually. Go to *Select > Similar* and Photoshop will automatically select all of the orange-colored areas of the image.

Next, go to *Layer > New > Layer via Copy* to create a new layer containing all of the orange areas. Rename this layer "Orange Glows."

245 The first thing that we'll do to this layer is apply a blur to create a glow effect around the signs. Go to *Filter > Blur > Gaussian Blur* and use a *Radius* of 35.5 pixels.

You can already see the effect of this blur layer, but we can really intensify it by changing its blending mode. Click on the blending mode drop-down menu in the *Layers* palette and select *Hard Light*. This has a similar effect to shining a bright light from behind the layer, and you'll immediately see the difference it makes.

246 With the Orange Glows layer selected, switch to the *Magic Wand* tool and set the mode to *Add to Selection*.

Zoom in on the sign with the blue Japanese lettering with an orange outline. Using the *Magic Wand* tool, select all of the orange areas on this sign. Next, go to *Select > Feather* and enter a *Feather Radius* of 2 pixels.

Go to *Layer > New > Layer via Copy* and rename the new layer "Orange Neons." Set this layer's blending mode to *Color Dodge* to create a bright yellow-orange glow.

We'll expand this glow a bit to make it look more like neon. Go to *Layer > Duplicate Layer* and accept the default name of "Orange Neons copy." Finally, go to *Filter > Blur > Gaussian Blur* and apply a *Radius* of 35.5 pixels to create a strong yellow glow around the letters.

247 The orange areas of the image are finished, so let's move onto the yellows. Click on the Background layer to select it, then zoom in on the area around the girl's left arm and the fox sign behind it.

Use the *Magic Wand* tool to select all of the yellow areas in this part of the image, then move over to the bird sign on the opposite side of the image and add the bird's eye to the selection.

248 Go to *Layer > New > Layer via Copy* to copy the yellow areas to a new layer, and rename the layer "Yellow Glows." Blur the layer by going to *Filter > Blur > Gaussian Blur* and entering a *Radius* of 25 pixels. Finally, set the layer's blending mode to *Screen* to brighten the glow a little.

249 Next, we will apply a neon glow to the green areas. Click on the Background layer in the *Layers* palette and zoom in on the cat sign.

Using the *Magic Wand* tool, select all of the green areas on the sign. Pan down to the bird sign, and select all of the green areas there, and on the sign above and to the right of it. Next, pan over to the top-right of the image and select the green border of the sign containing red Japanese characters.

Go to *Layer > New > Layer via Copy* and rename the new layer "Green Glows." Go to *Filter > Blur > Gaussian Blur* and set a *Radius* of 25 pixels, then change the layer's blending mode to *Hard Light*.

250 The green glows are a little weak at the moment, but we can fix this easily by duplicating the layer and therefore doubling the glow. Go to *Layer > Duplicate Layer* and accept the default name to immediately see the effect.

Next, we'll add a glow to the light blue areas. Click on the Background layer in the *Layers* palette, then use the *Magic Wand* tool to select the light blue petals in the bird sign. Then add the light blue border around the sign on the right with the blue and orange Japanese characters on it.

Go to *Layer > New > Layer via Copy*, and rename this new layer "Cyan Glows." Apply a *Gaussian Blur* of 25 pixels, and set the blending mode to *Screen*.

251 The glow effects are really beginning to bring the neon signs to life, but there are still a couple more colors that we want to add glows to before we're done.

First, we'll turn our attention to the reds. Click on the Background layer, and use the *Magic Wand* tool to select all of the red letters on the far right sign. Pan down the image and click on the three hanging red lanterns to add those to the selection, then pan across to the Stop sign on the left and add that to the selection.

Go to *Layer > New > Layer via Copy* to create a new layer containing a copy of the red parts of the image that we just selected. Rename this new layer "Red Glows." Apply the *Gaussian Blur* filter with a *Radius* of 25 pixels, then set the layer's blending mode to *Screen*.

252 Now we'll add a glow to the white areas. Click on the Background layer in the *Layers* palette.

Using the *Magic Wand* tool, click on all of the parts of the white letters on the hanging lanterns to begin your selection. Pan up to the fox sign and add the two white parts of the fox. Finally, pan all the way over to the cat sign at the top left of the image and add the white parts of the cat, including its eyes, to the selection.

Go to *Layer > New > Layer via Copy* and rename the new layer "White Glows." Apply a 25-pixel *Gaussian Blur* to this layer, and set its blending mode to *Screen*.

The white glows are a little overpowering at the moment, and they're drawing the eye away from the main focus of the image. We can tone them down a little by lowering the layer's opacity. This will make the layer fainter, allowing more of the background color to shine through. The *Opacity* setting is found at the top of the *Layers* palette. Change the layer's opacity to 80%.

253 That's our first set of neon glows finished, and it's a good time to save the image by going to *File > Save*.

With all of the glow layers complete, we'll do a bit of housekeeping and tidy up the *Layers* palette. Click on the *Create a New Group* icon at the bottom of the *Layers* palette, and rename the group "Neon Glows." Select all of the glow layers by Ctrl/Cmd+clicking on their names, and then drag them all into the Neon Glows group. When they're all in the group, click on the small arrow next to its name to collapse it and hide all the layers inside.

We'll now apply a slight blur to the background layer to help make the girl leap off the screen. Click on the Background layer and apply the *Gaussian Blur* filter with a *Radius* of 4.5 pixels. Zoom out so that you can see the whole image, and you will appreciate what a big difference this small change makes.

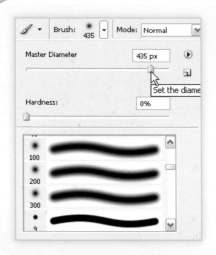

254 Next, we are going to add some warmer glow colors to the background. Instead of blurring selections like we did for the neon glows, we'll apply these warm glows by hand using the *Brush* tool.

Click on the Neon Glows group in the *Layers* palette, then click on the *Create a New Layer* icon and rename the new layer "Warm Glows." Set the blending mode of this new layer to *Hard Light*. Bring up the *Color Picker* and enter R: 253, G: 197, B: 137 to get a pastel orange color.

Click on the *Brush* tool in the *Toolbar*, and move to the *Tool Options* bar to change the settings. Click on the *Brush* drop-down menu, and pick the *Soft Round 300 Pixel* brush. Next, change the *Master Diameter* of this brush to 435 pixels. As you'll see, the reason we've chosen this figure is so that the brush is big enough to cover the hanging lanterns. The other brush options should be left at their default settings, as follows—*Mode: Normal, Opacity: 100%, Flow: 100%.*

255 Now everything's set up correctly, we can begin coloring. Zoom in on the red hanging lanterns and position the mouse over the top of the rightmost lantern.

Click once with the mouse and you will see a soft orange glow appear on the lantern, as if there were a light inside it. Do the same on the other two lanterns.

Let's add a few more glows. Pan left and click once at the top of the orange sign just under the girl's leg, then click once more at the top of the green sign next to it. Position the mouse over the girl's leg so that just a small amount of glow shines out from behind her.

Finally, pan over to the left a little more and click on the robin's breast and on the red hand of the Stop sign.

256 We'll now increase the brush size to add the next set of glows. Click on the *Brush* drop-down in the *Tool Options* bar and change the *Master Diameter* to 735 pixels.

For the first glow with this larger brush, move over to the cat sign at the top left of the image and click once in the center of the cat's face.

257 Zoom out so that you can see the whole of the image. We will add four more glows with this large brush to give the appearance of light glinting off the signs.

The first is in the top-right corner of the 70 speed sign. Position the brush so that a small crescent of light will appear above the sign, then click once. Do the same for the arrow sign and the top of the sign below it.

Finally, position the brush so its center is a little to the left of the girl's nose and click once to create a soft glow behind her head. You can see now why it was such a good idea to keep the girl on a separate layer. We can apply all sorts of effects to the background without affecting her at all.

258 There's one last set of warm glows to apply, and this time we'll use an even larger brush. Go to the *Brush* menu in the *Tool Options* bar and set the *Master Diameter* to 1255 pixels.

Position the brush over the girl's right wrist where it crosses her body and click once to apply a glow. Do the same at the top of the "g" sign, behind her right ankle, behind her right shoulder, and behind her head.

The glows are a little strong at the moment, so we can tone them down by setting the opacity of the Warm Glows layer to 75%. These glows not only add to the neon background effects, but they also help to lift the girl out from the background.

259 That's all of the glow areas finished, so it's a good time to save your image. The next thing that we are going to focus on is the sky.

Click on the Background layer in the *Layers* palette to select it. Switch to the *Magic Wand* tool, and carefully click on each of the areas of the sky in turn to create one large selection. You may need to zoom in a little to select the smaller areas around the flags and the girl's hair. Don't forget to add the two small areas between her arm and her boot.

With the selection complete, go to *Layer > New > Layer via Copy* and rename the new layer "Sky Effect 1." Apply a *Gaussian Blur* of 80 pixels to this layer to give it a large, soft glow, then change the layer's blending mode to *Screen*.

260 We're getting closer to the glowing effect that we want for the sky, but there's still a way to go. First, let's double the glowing effect by duplicating the layer.

Make sure that the Sky Effect 1 layer is selected in the *Layers* palette, and go to *Layer > Duplicate Layer*. Give the new layer the name "Sky Effect 2." The effect is a bit too strong because the layer is automatically set to *Screen* mode, but we can alter it by changing the blending mode to *Hard Light*.

261 The sky is looking good now, but it still looks slightly removed from the rest of the image. We want the glow from the sky to be shining down into the street to tie the two parts of the image together.

The simplest way to do this is to increase the size of the glow that we have already created. Go to *Edit > Transform > Scale* to bring up a transform box around the sky. You can drag the square handles at the sides and corners of the box to resize the sky.

First, drag the bottom-left corner handle down and to the left until it's about level with the bottom of the fire hydrant. The glow is encroaching a little too far over the signs on the left, so click inside the transform box and drag the sky shape to the right. Finally, click the bottom-center handle and drag it down to increase the size of the glow a little more. You don't need to be too precise with this, just pull the handles until the sky is in a position that you're happy with. When you're done, press Enter on the keyboard to apply the transformation.

262 The new sky glow still has a bit too much definition, so we'll blur it some more. Go to *Filter > Blur > Gaussian Blur* and apply a *Radius* of 80 pixels. Save the image.

We'll now do a bit more work on the girl. Click on the arrow beside the Girl group in the *Layers* palette to open the group, then click on Girl Layer to select it. Go to *Layer > Duplicate Layer* and keep the default name of "Girl Layer copy."

Change the layer's blending mode to *Screen* to lighten the layer. We don't want it to be quite that bright, so change the layer's opacity to 50% by entering that figure into the *Opacity* box at the top of the *Layers* palette. Finally, apply a *Gaussian Blur* with a *Radius* of 1.5 pixels to the layer.

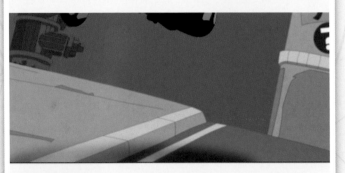

263 If you zoom in on the girl's face, you'll notice that there is a thin black line separating the two pink tones. We want to remove this line so that the black lines only represent the outlines of areas in the image.

Select Girl Layer in the *Layers* palette, then go to *Filter > Noise > Median*. The *Median* filter reduces noise in an image by blending and smoothing the brightness between different areas. Set the *Radius* to 5 pixels and click *OK*.

If you look closely at the image now, you'll notice that the black line has gone.

264 The girl is almost finished now, but the picture still looks a little flat. We can really make it look like the girl is leaping into the air by adding a shadow beneath her. There is a convention in cartooning (probably just because it's quicker to draw) that shadows under leaping figures are represented by a simple ellipse rather than an anatomically correct shape. We can achieve this by using the *Elliptical Marquee* tool.

Click on the Background layer in the *Layers* palette. Select the *Elliptical Marquee* tool from the *Toolbar*, and set the following options in the *Tool Options* bar: *Mode: New Selection*, *Feather*: 0 px, *Anti-alias*: checked. Zoom out of the image so that you can see the gray border area below it. Click in the bottom left of the image and drag right and down outside the image area to create a shape like the one shown.

Go to *Layer > New > Layer via Copy*, and rename the new layer "Girl Shadow." Next, set the blending mode of the layer to *Multiply*. You will notice that the area becomes darker. Now, we just need to soften the shadow. Go to *Filter > Blur > Gaussian Blur* and set a *Radius* of 50 pixels, then click *OK*.

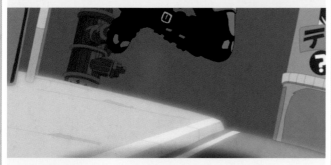

265 The shadow's given the girl a bit more lift, but we can give the image an even more three-dimensional quality by lightening the ground around the shadow.

Zoom in closer to the sidewalk and road, then select the Background layer in the *Layers* palette. We'll make a manual selection of the road area using the *Polygonal Lasso* tool, so select it from the *Toolbar*. Make sure that *Feather* is set to 0 px and *Anti-alias* is checked in the *Tool Options* bar. Click at the edge of the sidewalk area to start the selection, then work your way around the sidewalk and road area, clicking every time you need to turn a corner (don't worry if it's not perfect). When you get back to where you started, the small circle will appear next to the cursor icon meaning that the next time you click, the selection will be complete.

Go to *Layer > New > Layer via Copy* and rename the new layer "Sidewalk Highlight." Set the blending mode of the layer to *Screen*, then go to *Filter > Blur > Gaussian Blur* and set a *Radius* of 40 pixels to soften the Sidewalk Highlight layer.

266 The highlight is good, but it's a bit too strong in places. Luckily, because it's on a separate layer, we can simply use the *Eraser* to blend the highlight into the background.

Select the *Eraser* tool from the *Toolbar*. We need to adjust some of the settings in the *Tool Options* bar to the following: *Mode: Brush*, *Opacity: 100%, Flow: 55%*, and select a soft brush with a *Master Diameter* of 1255 pixels.

Click once on the sidewalk area near the base of each of the speed and Stop signs. Click again at the base of the fire hydrant, and then one final time in the bottom-right corner of the selection.

267 Now that we've added some modeling to the sidewalk and road, we should do the same to some of the other areas of the image. We'll start by adding some highlights to the signposts to make them look more 3D.

Move to the speed and arrow signs on the left side of the image. Create a new layer in the *Layers* palette called "Posts Highlights." Switch to the *Polygonal Lasso* tool and make a selection on the right side of the biggest signpost. We'll break the selection into sections, so first, start from the top of the sign and create a rectangular selection down to the first join in the post. Switch to *Add to Selection* mode in the *Tool Options* bar, and create a similar-shaped selection in the second segment of the post. Finally for the large post, create a thin horizontal selection along the top of the first bracket.

Next, turn your attention to the smaller post with the signs attached to it. Create two selections on this post—one thin selection on the right side above the signs, and one small selection directly below the signs. Finally, create a selection on the stop light just below the arrow sign, and extend it onto the heel of the girl's boot.

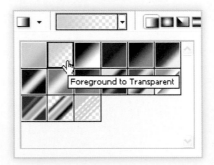

269 Click near the top of the image, about halfway across it, and drag the gradient to the left of the girl's right boot. The gradient will appear when you release the mouse. To turn the gradient into a bright highlight, we'll change the layer's blending mode. Go to the *Layers* palette and change the Sidewalk Highlight layer's blending mode to *Screen*. Finally, deselect the selection by pressing Ctrl/Cmd+D.

The edges are still a bit harsh on the highlights, so go to *Filter > Blur > Gaussian Blur* and set the *Radius* to 10 pixels.

268 Now that we have made our selection, we need to fill it. We'll use the *Gradient* tool here to give a transition from light to dark. We want the gradient to run from our selected color to the post's current color, so we'll use a *Foreground to Transparent* gradient. We'll keep the same orange color as we used before (RGB settings R: 253, G: 197, B: 137).

Foreground to Transparent

Next, select the *Gradient* tool from the *Toolbar* and click on the drop-down menu in the *Tool Options* bar to select *Foreground to Transparent*. You should also make sure that the other settings in the *Tool Options* bar are correct, as follows: *Mode*: *Normal*, *Opacity*: 100%, *Reverse*: unchecked, *Dither*: checked, *Transparency*: checked.

270 The highlights are still a little too strong on the signs. Switch to the *Eraser* tool and change the *Master Diameter* of the brush to 333 pixels.

Erase the bottom of the lower vertical highlight on the first signpost, and then the bottom of the upper highlight on the second signpost.

Once this is done, apply another *Gaussian Blur* with a *Radius* of 10 pixels.

271 We'll now add some highlights to the building on the right side, next to the poster with the girl's face on it.

Create a new layer to store this highlight and rename it "Building Highlights." Switch to the *Polygonal Lasso* tool and create a thin selection along the side of the building, starting at the bottom of the fox sign and finishing at around level with the center of the question mark sign.

Make sure that you are in *Add to Selection* mode, then make another selection along the edge of the line of bricks running across the building. Select an area about three-quarters of the length of the line of bricks.

272 We'll now create a gradient across the selection.

Switch to the *Gradient* tool and keep the same options as we used in step 268.

Drag a gradient running from just beneath the center hanging lantern to the middle of the cheek of the girl in the poster.

Deselect the selection and apply a *Gaussian Blur* of 10 pixels to the layer. Finally, change the layer's blending mode to *Hard Light*.

273 We're almost at the end now. First, let's soften the edges of those building highlights in the same way as we did for the signposts.

Click on the *Eraser* tool in the *Toolbar* and keep it at the same settings that we used previously. Gently brush away the top, bottom, and right edge of the large highlight to leave a thin strip, then erase a small amount of the lower highlight.

275 That's it, the image is complete! As a last measure of good housekeeping, we'll tidy up the *Layers* palette.

Create a new group and rename it "Background Effects." Select the Sky Effects 2, Sky Effects 1, Building Highlights, Posts Highlights, and Sidewalk Highlights layers by Ctrl/Cmd+clicking on their names, and drag them into the Background Effects group.

Next, drag the Warm Glows layer into the Neon Glows group, and drag the Girl Shadow layer into the Girl group. Click the arrow next to any open groups in the *Layers* palette to close them. Finally, save your file.

Congratulations for making it this far. Hopefully you are happy with the results of your efforts, and you're now the proud owner of a fully colored manga image. We hope that you've enjoyed coloring it and that you've learned a lot of new and useful Photoshop skills along the way.

Now you can go back to the beginning and try some new color schemes and effects of your own!

274 There's one final adjustment that we'll make to the overall image. We'll use Photoshop's *Levels* command to adjust the color balance of the background, making the dark areas darker and the light areas a little lighter.

Photoshop's *Levels* dialog box is a very useful tool for fine-tuning the appearance of your images. It can look a little complex, but the image updates whenever you make an adjustment, so you can easily see the effect that your alterations will have before you apply them.

Click on the Background layer in the *Layers* palette, then go to *Image > Adjustments > Levels* to open the *Levels* dialog box. By moving the small black arrow underneath the histogram, you can increase the contrast in the dark areas of the image. Drag the arrow right until the first *Input Levels* box reads 30, then click *OK*. The new color balance improves the mood and dynamism of the image.

Input Levels: 30 | 1.00 | 255

Output Levels: 0 | 255